The Victory Monument

Sculptor: Leonard Crunelle

Architect: John A. Nyden

The white and bronze Victory Monument is the most famous land-mark of Chicago's African-American community. It was erected by the State of Illinois and the South Park Commission in 1927 to honor the African American soldiers of World War I, following a lengthy campaign led by the *Chicago Defender.*

The soldiers had been formed as the Eighth Regiment of the Illinois National Guard, but when the U.S. entered the war, the regiment was reorganized as the 370th U.S. Infantry of the 93rd Division. It saw service on the war's major French battlefields and was especially distinguished as the last regiment pursuing the retreating German forces in the Aisne-Marne region just before the Armistice on November 11, 1918.

Around the monument's shaft are bronze panels finished with a rich black patination. There are three life-size figures in relief: a soldier, a woman representing motherhood, and the figure of "Columbia" holding a tablet listing the regiment's principal battles. The model for the soldier was Ozzie Levels, a sergeant in the Eighth Regiment. The fourth panel lists the names of the soldiers who died in battle. In 1936, the bronze "doughboy" was added to the top of the column.

The sculptor of the bronze, Leonard Crunelle, was born in France in a coal-mining town near Lens that was destroyed in World War I. He was a student of noted Chicago sculptor Lorado Taft. The granite column and architectural setting of the monument were a collaborative design of Crunelle and Chicago architect John Nyden.

The Victory Monument:

The

Beacon

Of Chicago's Bronzeville

By:

Dempsey J. Travis

Urban Research Press, Inc.

URBAN RESEARCH PRESS, INC.

WWW.URBANRESEARCHPRESS.COM

Library of Congress Cataloging-in-Publication Data.

Travis, Dempsey J.
The Victory Monument: The Beacon Of Chicago's Bronzeville
Bibliography: P
Includes index
1. United States Armed Forces - Afro-Americans in Military - History.

Dedicated To:

All soldiers who fought in both World War I and World War II to make democracy a reality at home and abroad.

This book is also dedicated to the Chicago Military Academy Cadets who will graduate in the Class of 2003, and those leaders in the next millennium who will follow them.

Other books by
Dempsey J. Travis

Views From The Back Of The Bus During WWII And Beyond
The Life and Times of Redd Foxx
An Autobiography of Black Jazz
The Duke Ellington Primer
The Louis Armstrong Odyssey: From Jane Alley To
        America's Jazz Ambassador
I Refuse To Learn To Fail

For additional books by the author:

www.urbanresearchpress.com

INTRODUCTION

The Old Eighth Regiment Armory, a military installation, was tucked in the midst of modest homes built before the turn of the century at 35th and Giles (Forest) Avenue. The storied Eighth Illinois Infantry Armory became a centerpiece of community activity from the day it first opened in 1915. The area became known as Bronzeville in the early 1930s. It was located just a short distance from many symbols of the rich Negro history in Chicago's "Black Belt". Thirty-Fifth Street was Black America's Broadway with its theaters and cabarets. The Armory was less than a block away from the Sunset Cafe/Grand Terrace where Louis Armstrong, Earl Hines, Cab Calloway and Fletcher Henderson made their initial steps toward the Hall of Musical Fame.

Two blocks East of the Armory on 35th Street was South Parkway (which in the 1920s was Grand Boulevard) and the home of the Supreme Liberty Life Insurance Company and the Victory Monument which stood in the center of the Boulevard in memory of the Black Soldiers who died in World War I. Several blocks West of the Eighth Regiment on State Street was the Binga State Bank which was organized in 1908 by Jesse Binga, a Black entrepreneur and on the same block was the Douglas National Bank founded in 1922 by Anthony Overton another business pioneer. State Street was considered Black America's Wall Street.

The immense dimensions of the Eighth Armory served as meeting hall, revival center, and a dance ballroom featuring such orchestras as Duke Ellington, Fletcher Henderson, Fats Waller, Jimmie Lunceford and Benny Goodman. The Armory was a community hub when it was not being used for its primary role as Headquarters for the Units of Black Troops of the Illinois National Guard, The Eighth Illinois Infantry, the 1st and 2nd Battalion of the 178th Infantry Regiment, and the 184th Field Artillery Battalion, all of whom were bloodied in battles in both the States and abroad.

The Old Eighth Regiment Armory was a scarred but proud Old Building when it put its imprint on my life. The time in point was February, 1946. I was a 1st Lieutenant who became inactive after returning from active service in World War II. After completing Law School, I resumed my military career by rejoining my old unit, the 184th Field Artillery Battalion, which was still headquartered in the Old Eighth Regiment Armory.

I

Every Tuesday on Drill night you would find me at the Armory, but my visits were not confined to just Drill night, thus it was not unusual for me to stop by the Armory three or four nights a week to keep track of how the unit was progressing. The 8th Armory was my home from 1948 until it moved in the early 1960s to the Armory at 51st and Cottage Grove. Because of the downsizing of the peacetime army the Armory was closed. For some 30 years the Old Eighth Armory lay dormant and unattended. It deteriorated into a useless, large empty structure and a neighborhood eyesore until the Chicago Board of Education under the guidance of Mayor Richard M. Daley, Gery Chico, President and Paul E. Vallas, Chief Executive Officer acquired it in December, 1997.

The Chicago Board of Education is establishing a Military High School Academy in the remodeled Old Eighth Armory and adding an annex, at a cost of $18. 5 million dollars. The facility is scheduled to open for students on the 14th day of August, 1999.

This new educational concept gives great hope to the community of Bronzeville and the City of Chicago. There is no question that that storied building will again become one of the cornerstones in a revitalization and restoration of a historical, proud community. The restored facility, as an Educational Center, will serve as a lamp of learning in that it will provide the youths from every section of the City with the training and secondary education needed to become economic contributors and leaders in the new millennium.

Earl E. Strayhorn
Lieutenant Colonel A. U. S. (Retired)
Presiding Judge 1st Municipal District Circuit Court of Cook County (Retired)

Contents

he old *The Eighth Regiment Armory* (above), and the new *The Eighth Regiment
rmory Bronzeville Military Academy* located at 3515-33 South Giles Avenue,
hicago, Illinois.

Chapter I
From "Black Belt" Sandlots of the Ghetto to the Battlefields of the World

Following the Civil War of the 1860s and the Great Chicago Fire of 1871, there was a group of Colored Ex-Union soldiers who could still hear the echo of the wake up calls of the bugle boy blowing reveille in their ears.

The moonlight patriots were barred from membership in the Illinois State Militia because of the melanin in their skin. Thus, they organized their own military platoons of boys in blue and named themselves the Hannibal (247-183 B.C.) Guards in honor of North Africa's great carthaginian general.

The Hannibal Guards changed their name after a very brief period in an effort to appease the white military establishment that continued to exclude them. Thus, they became the Cadets, a term that did not have the threatening sting of Black militancy.

In an effort to remove the stench of absolute racism from President Abraham Lincoln's Militia by the Lake, Alderman Martin B. Madden who later became the Congressman of the First District in Chicago, Illinois aided Major John Buckner, his most trusted Black political recruiter in a successful effort to get state funds for an all Black regiment. Buckner was the sole Black member of the Illinois House of Representatives in 1894, he was figuratively the father of the Eighth Infantry Regiment.

The Afro-American platoons consisted of sandlot soldiers in search of a home. Shelter for the Black Army volunteers became evident with the laying of the cornerstone for the permanent headquarters for the Eighth Regiment Illinois National Guard Armory. The ceremony for the new building took place on Sunday, October 11, 1914 at high noon. This was an event of national importance because

2

*Congressman Martin B. Madden of the
1st District in Illinois.*

*State Representative John Buckner, the
only Black in the Statehouse.*

it was the first such occurrence to take place in an escalating climate
of racial prejudice and interracial friction following the reconstruc-
tion period of the late nineteenth century. Up until 1915 the Eighth
Regiment headquarters had been in a livery stable and their parade
grounds were sandlots and city streets.

Twenty years earlier a Black Infantry Company in Chicago was
legitimized at the command of President Grover Cleveland's,
Secretary of War Daniel S. Lamont on November 4, 1895 and placed
under the leadership of Captain Robert R. Jackson, a Black man. The
company was mustered into federal service and made a part of the
Ninth Battalion during the Spanish-American War and shipped out to
Santiago, Cuba a neighbor 90 miles southeast of the State of Florida.
This group of men were basically the origin of the Eighth Infantry

Sergeant Major C.A. Fleetwood of the
4th U.S. Colored Troops in the Civil War
won the Congressional Medal of Honor.

Sergeant George H. Watson, Congressional
Medal of Honor winner for heroic service
rendered during the Spanish-American War
in Cuba.

Regiment, and they went to war as volunteers, the same as their
fathers had in the Civil War. The company was garrisoned and performed guard duty on the island of Cuba during the four year recon-
struction period. Following the war with Spain over Cuba, the Black
company from Chicago was mustered out of federal service on March
16, 1899.

The Eighth Infantry Illinois National Guard celebrated its fif-
teenth anniversary on Thursday November 3, 1910 with a grand reception and ball at the Seventh Regiment Armory a white military establishment located at 34th Street and Wentworth Avenue. The friends of
the regiment committed themselves to making this the biggest inte-

Colonel Franklin A. Denison, the second highest ranking Colored officer in the United States Army during World War I.

grated social event to be given in the history of Chicago by people of color. Admission to the gala was fifty cents.

    The officers and men of the Eighth Illinois Infantry were mobilized again under a directive from President Woodrow Wilson's Secretary of War, Lindley M. Garrison on June 19, 1916 and mustered into federal service June 30, 1916. They served under the command of Colonel Franklin A. Denison at the Mexican border. They were mustered out of the service four months later on October 27, 1916.

    The men of the Eighth Regiment returned to Chicago at 9:00 A.M. on October 28, 1916 in triumph. They paraded through the Loop district and down south State Street (the Black Broadway of America) enroute to their newly constructed armory at 35th and Forest (Giles). A huge number of spectators stood shoulder to shoulder and sidewalk deep on both sides of the street. The sight of the brown doughboys brought tears, cheers and shouts of joy that were

DOWN WITH TAXES

me of the Eighth Illinois Officers led the regiment in a parade down State Street after urning from the Mexican border conflict on October 28, 1916. The crowd of people was mense, cheers and shouts of joy rang out from both sides of the street.

almost deafening from both the pedestrians and those individuals waving the red, white and blue flag of the forty-eight states as they leaned dangerously out of their second and third floor windows.

The returning chocolate soldiers paraded proudly through the city streets. They were led by a platoon of Eighth Infantry Officers who were mounted on horses. The officers and men were greeted at the armory by the Mayor William Hale Thompson, Judge Scully, Congressman Martin B. Madden and Alderman Oscar DePriest who in 1915 replaced Madden in the Chicago City Council, and thus, was the first Black member of that body. DePriest was subsequently elected to Congress after Madden died suddenly in Washington, D.C. in 1928.

The election of Oscar DePriest to the United States Congress

Chicago's Mayor William H. Thompson, a Republican, served three terms with almost 100% support from the Negro communities.

Oscar DePriest, Alderman of Chicago's Second Ward was the Mayor's walking delegate in the Colored districts.

marked the first Negro Congressman to be elected in the Twentieth Century. Politically for the first four decades of the Twentieth Century, Blacks had only one voice in Congress, and that was Congressman Oscar DePriest. His election symbolized the political development of Negroes in Chicago.

Also present at the homecoming ceremony for the Eighth Regiment were a number of Colored societies and Fraternal Orders, such as The Masons, The Pythians, The Elks, The Foresters, and numerous other public minded civic organizations.

The Eighth Regiment was a political and social vehicle for a body of 2000 men of color who volunteered to join the army and val-

large crowd gathered in front of the new Eighth Regiment Armory at 35th Street and 'orest (Giles) waiting to welcome the brown doughboys home on a pleasant October morning in 1916.

idate their right to full citizenship. Members of the regiment were gung ho on being called to active duty for World War I on July 25, 1917. It was the belief among Blacks at that time that if you fought in a war and paid real estate taxes, you would be treated like other Americans. That hypothesis was not true because racism is epidemic and more than skin deep. The regiment was subsequently federalized on August 3, and placed under the command of Colonel Franklin A. Denison, a tall, dashing, civic and social leader from the "Black Belt"area on the Southeast side of Chicago.

Following an intensive warfare training session, the Regiment was redesignated the 370th Infantry of the 93rd Division on

The doughboys came marching home on February 17, 1919. Top photo: South Michigan Boulevard. Bottom photo: The Coliseum at 14th Street and Wabash.

French Officers shown pinning 170 Croix de Guerre or The Legion of Honor medals for gallantry in action, on the chest of Chicago's Black heroes. The United States Army did not give a single Black soldier The Congressional Medal of Honor for heroic service during World War I.

December 1, 1917. It was the only regiment in the United States Army that was one hundred percent Black from head to toe, from the rank of colonel to buck private.

Upon arriving in France the 370th was involved in many hard fought battles against the Germans (Huns). Some of the most publicized engagements were fought side by side with the French Army at the Argonne Forest, St. Gobain Forest, the Oise-Aisne offensive and the Lorraine offensive.

On November 5, 1918 the battle on the western front became so fierce that the Germans began to retreat on the double. The Afro-American Regiment was ordered to pursue the "Huns" to the end of the earth. On November 7, the battalion moved up and passed Bosmont, Tarveaux, Virginette, Lambercy, Mont Plaiair, and on to the front lines at the Rue Larcher. The battalion reached its objective at Gue d' Hossus, Belgium moments before the Armistice was signed on

November 11, 1918.

The Germans in fits of terror nicknamed the dashing Afro-American soldiers to whom death appeared to mean nothing, the "Black Devils" whereas their friendly French allies in arms referred to them as "Partridges" because of their proud, ramrod bearing.

Under fire the 370th conducted themselves in a manner that was above and beyond the call of duty. However, the regiment left one hundred twenty-eight of its fighting doughboys resting under white grave markers in France's Flanders Field. Five hundred ninety-eight of the fighting men of the 370th were hospitalized for wounds received on the battlefront. The United States did not honor any of the Blacks with the Medal of Honor in WWI. However, the French who fought in the trenches with Black soldiers awarded over 170 breathing Blacks with the French Croix de Guerre or the Legion of Honor for gallantry in action.

The welcome that the 370th Regiment received on its return to Chicago on February 17, 1919 eclipsed any event given to a regiment in the history of the city. Upon their arrival at daybreak on that cold and snowy February morning, following their detainment they found themselves surrounded by thousands of admirers, relatives and new found friends who were on hand to greet them at the 12th Street Illinois Central Railroad Station. Spontaneous, uncontrollable outbursts of joy prevailed in the adjacent snow covered Grant Park which was just one hundred feet north of the train station. The kissing, hugging and handshaking continued until the bugle sounded for the men to fall in line for their parade through the heart of the city enroute to the spacious Coliseum at 14th and Wabash Avenue where twenty-two thousand admirers occupied every available foot of space within the walls of the giant size convention hall while awaiting their arrival. An additional thirty thousand individuals attempted to storm the fortress-like building entrance for admittance to see their heroes. No program could be rendered, although the welcoming committee had planned one.

Though the embattled warriors had been literally smothered with affection by the grateful French, the City of Chicago put the icing on the cake. The march down Michigan Boulevard through the busi-

Captain Lloyd G. Wheeler, II who served in France with the 370th during World War I. He is remembered by his Chicago friends as a strutting dandy and uncle of Lloyd G Wheeler, III the last president of the Supreme Liberty Life Insurance Company.

ness section of the city required more self control than even well disciplined soldiers could handle. Little Black children, old men and women, everyone in sight gave vent to their emotions. The Colored children at Haven Elementary School at 15th and Wabash were the only ones excused from class to see the Colored soldiers; in contrast the entire school system closed down when the white veterans came marching home.

During the parade of the chocolate soldiers, the police protection crumbled like soda crackers in a bowl of soup because an out of hand holiday atmosphere prevailed. Friends and relatives rushed the lines of the parade and a would be orderly march eventually melted like ice cream on a hot summer day.

The Windy City welcome exceeded the Black warriors' wildest dreams. The men were overjoyed with the ribbons of affection that Chicago had wrapped around them. Thus, they felt that the hardships they had endured on the European battlefields had not been in vain.

Herbert Young, a World War I veteran who died in New York City on April 22, 1999 at the age of 112, said: *"The U.S. Army did not want them in the infantry because they were Colored. Therefore, they were relegated to fight under the French flag."*

Colonel Charles Young, the soldier who should have been made a general.

Racism hovered over the heads of Negro Army Officers like vultures circling above the dying and the dead. The military establishment believed that the Army would be best served by having Black troops placed under the paternal eyes of white officers.

Colonel Charles Young, was the highest ranking Negro officer in the Army and the third soldier of color to graduate from the West Point Academy in 1889. He was the first to feel the hot flames of overt and cruel racism. In spite of the fact that he had served with distinction under General Pershing in the military action on the Mexican border. He was the logical officer to take command of a Negro division. Despite his futile efforts to prove his fitness by riding horseback from Ohio to Washington, D.C., he was forcefully retired from the service as being unfit.

Colonel Franklin A. Denison the commanding officer of the 370th Infantry (formerly the 8th Illinois National Guard) like Colonel Young was also relieved of duty for being physically unfit. A

Left, Colonels Franklin A. Denison, Roberts and Otis T. Duncan of the "Black Devils".

Black General was not in America's well stacked deck of cards. Most of

Extreme right front row, 1st Lieutenant Binga Desmond, nephew of Jessie Binga, the Chicago banker, and other officers of the 370th.

the other Negro Field Officers remained unassigned for the duration of World War I.

In the field, racism against Negro officers was manifested in a variety of ways. The late Charles Houston, Dean of Howard University Law School and a former First Lieutenant of the 368th Infantry, 92nd Division, wrote in the Pittsburgh Courier: *The hate and scorn heaped upon us Negro officers by American whites, at Camp Mencou and Vanmei, in France convinced me there was no sense of dying in a world ruled by a point of view that treated us less than equals. They isolated us off from our fellow white officers. They made us eat on benches in order to maintain segregation and destroyed any prestige we had left in front of the French officers.*

The 40,000 members of the Ku Klux Klan on parade in Washington, D.C. five years after World War I.

Chapter II

The Battle For Black Liberation Ignited Bombs and Fires Following World War I

T he Chicago race riot during the red hot summer of 1919 was one of many that scorched the land and smeared the sidewalks of the cities with blood.

The northern front line warriors against equality of the races were for the most part teenagers and white war vets with Ku Klux Klan mentality and determined to convince Black ex-servicemen that President Abraham Lincoln's, City by the Lake was not the Arc de Triomphe in Paris, France. The white man's jobs, housing, and pale face white women were off-limits. To punctuate their point, Negro men were frequently brutalized, lynched, shot and stoned to death as a reminder to all Colored people that America was the white man's domain.

Although the Illinois Eighth Infantry Regiment was mustered into service to fight in the Spanish American War, the Mexican Border skirmish and World War I, they were not thought of as having the right kind of stuff to defend their own community during the "Blood Red Summer" of 1919. White troops from the Ninth, Tenth and Eleventh Infantry of Illinois were singularly mustered into service to perform the task of protecting the Black community during the bloody July of 1919 by Illinois Governor Frank O. Lowden who was persuaded by Mayor William "Big Bill" Thompson to send in 6,200 troops. The major employers of a large number of Black workers had put pressure on the Mayor to stop the destruction.

The incident that sparked the riot on July 27, 1919 was the murder of teenage Eugene Williams a January 30, 1919 graduate of the Raymond Elementary School at 3663 South Wabash. The lad was killed by rocks thrown by some white thugs who felt that their inalienable rights were infringed upon because the Black kid had accidently

The January 1919 Raymond Elementary School 3663 South Wabash graduation picture of Eugene Williams, the initial riot victim of Chicago's "Blood Red" summer. Williams is the first person on the extreme right in the third row.

The beginning of the Chicago race riot in 1919. Whites and Negroes leave the Twenty-ninth Street Beach after Eugene Williams had drowned as the result of a stoning.

A mob armed with bricks in search of a Negro.

The white mob caught a Negro and stoned him to death.

The arrival of the police after the fact.

A bomb was thrown into a building at 3365 South Indiana Avenue occupied by Negroes. A six year old child was killed.

floated his homemade raft across the imaginary Color line in Lake Michigan offshore at the 29th Street beach.

On July 28, 1919 the second day of the Chicago riot, a Nigger hating white mob from the near Southwest side invaded Bronzeville. When some of the returning veterans of the Eighth Regiment got word of the white boys' plans, they rallied around a battle cry that they had learned in France, "Il ne passeront pas" ("They shall not pass").

The white mob was turned back at 35th and Wentworth when confronted by the heavily armed Black veterans who were still wearing their Army uniforms. When common sense kicked in, the hooligans hastily retreated west back to Halsted Street and out of range of the weapons being displayed by the Black doughboys.

Today there is a monument in the center parkway of Dr.

Negro stockyard workers cut off from work because of the riots pick up their checks at a temporary pay station in the Colored Y.M.C.A. at 3763 South Wabash Avenue.

Martin Luther King Drive (formerly Grand Boulevard and later South Parkway) at 35th Street. To those who visit the monument, it is seen as a tribute to Black soldiers who served in World War I. However, to the old timers, it symbolizes the routing of that white mob in the 1919 riot.

In May 1919 preceding the July race riot Richard B. Harrison, the famous Broadway stage actor's home at 3624 South Grand Boulevard (Dr. Martin Luther King Drive) was fire-bombed. His house was targeted as one of a series of destructive acts directed at Black-occupied buildings. His home was subsequently purchased and occupied by Ida B. Wells, the fearless civil rights activist. The expanding of the "Black Belt" could be measured by the bombings between July 1, 1917 and March 1, 1921. The bombing of homes in ethnic changing neighborhoods occurred on an average of once every fifteen days. Two bombings a month is a large number for a Black population numbering 100,000.

Five weeks before the full fledged riot broke out on July 27, 1919 some Back of the Yards hoodlums killed two Blacks on a streetcar enroute home from work at the meat packing plant of Armour and Company, which was located in the heart of the stockyard district, adjacent to the other giant butchers of the world, Swift and Company and the Wilson Company. Meat packing companies were located in an area bounded by 39th Street on the north and 47th Street on the south. The east boundary of the stockyards was Halsted and the west boundary was Ashland. The Chicago Stockyards employed more Blacks than any other single industry in the city. During the riot some Blacks were locked in if they were at work when the riot started whereas, others trying to get to work were locked out because they had to travel through the turf of the Back of the Yards street gangs such as the Ragen Colts.

The late Congressman William L. Dawson, who was a young First Lieutenant just returning from World War I, digested and regurgitated a great deal of the anti-Black propaganda of the Hyde Park-Kenwood Property Owners' Association. He also witnessed the rivers of blood flowing down the avenues during the summer of 1919.

Dawson made the following statement about the activity of Oscar DePriest, the former Alderman in the 1919 race riot:

> *What great admiration I had for Oscar DePriest a light skin man who really had guts. I remember seeing him put on a policeman's cap and uniform and drive a paddy wagon into the stockyards to bring out the Negroes who were trapped inside during the riot of 1919. He was highly respected as a former alderman, and he did what not a single policeman had the courage to do. Again and again he went into the stockyards, bringing Negroes out with him*

Milk was supplied for babies by the Red Cross for the duration of the riot.

William L. Dawson, World War I veteran and future Alderman and Congressman.

in the paddy wagon until finally he had rescued a large number of them from the white mob. His courageous action, undertaken at great personal risk, moved me to do something which taught me a lesson and something I rarely have done since. I sat down and wrote Oscar a letter.

I told him I thought he had performed a great heroic deed and that I personally wanted to congratulate him. I also told him that he could always depend upon me for support in

*anything he would undertake in the future and
that I was ready to stand beside him. Some
years later that letter turned up to my embar-
rassment. Oscar and I were then on the oppo-
site sides of the fence politically, but he
remembered that letter and dug it up and used
it against me, referring to it in his speeches and
waving it before his audiences wherever he
went.*

Anna Mary Grinnell who died two decades ago at age 96 told
the author that she and her husband owned a bakery at 3308 South
State. They spent the night of July 29, 1919 lying on the floor dodg-
ing bullets being fired by whites from the open windows of their
speeding cars as they raced up and down south State Street.

Mrs. Grinnell said that one car with four white occupants with
guns blazing raced passed her store at 33rd Street. She later learned
that by the time the hoodlums reached 35th Street all four had been
killed. The Blacks had set up army-like barricades to keep their community out of harm's way.

The Grinnells spent anxious hours on July 30th trying to figure out a way to get their young daughter out of town to a safe haven.
Blacks were unable to travel north of 16th Street to get to the Polk
Street train stations. The white man who delivered flour to their bakery offered to take Mrs. Grinnell and the child to the train depot, but
he would not come south of 16th Street because he was afraid of the
Blacks. So Mr. Grinnell tried to make arrangements to get his wife and
child to 16th Street, where the friendly flour man could meet them
and escort them to an eastbound train for Youngstown, Ohio. But
before the arrangements could be made, the riot ended.

The human cost of the riot was the lives of thirty-eight men
and boys including twenty-three Blacks. Five hundred and thirty seven
people were injured; three-hundred and forty-two of that number
were Black.

World War I recruits practice marching in Grant Park. Note the Art Institute in the background.

Chapter III

Excerpts From World War I Letters With Noxious Racial Views

C harles L. Samson an Army First Lieutenant offers some insight from a white man's point of view on World War I for the period between October 1917 to July 1919. He was a mechanical engineer from Chicago, and served as an Officer in the Engineer Corps from 1917 until his discharge, in July 1919.

In approximately 250 letters that he sent to his wife, Lieutenant Samson gives frank opinions on many topics concerning his military experiences. Topics such as: a description of his training experience and camp life at Fort Leavenworth, Kansas and at Camp Meade, Maryland; his brief stay in England; and service in France, where he served as a Commanding Officer of a Chinese labor company. (Militarily speaking, the Chinese did little during the war, but they contributed about 200,000 laborers, who served in France under French, British and American supervision.) Lt. Samson did not see combat duty during the war.

Although many of Lt. Samson's remarks are highly critical of his fellow servicemen, the Chinese laborers he supervised, the French people and their customs, he furnished a vivid expression of one soldier's viewpoint about the war, its participants, and situations.

October 27, 1917

> *The 1st Co. subscribed $16,000 for liberty war bonds. A fat rich Jewish 2nd Lieutenant subscribed for $10,000 of it.*
>
> *It seems like a long long time since I left Chicago. Although it has been just one month*

but I assure you I was never so hustled, crowded and literally jammed through a month in my life. About 60% of the men here are said to be members of a Masonic Lodge. I daily find new men from Illinois. The instructor who uses such mangled English and speaks nigger dialect is from the University of Texas. We also have a member of the rich John Randolph family from Roanoke, Virginia. He is a good student but a snob.

October 29, 1917

Criticism of Jewish merchant in Leavenworth: On the hike today I found that the bunch uniformly resented the remarks of our Hebrew friend from Leavenworth. The refrain of his remarks was 'we are behind you.' The interpretation of the bunch was 'we are behind you getting your jobs.'

December 14, 1917

The West Point Cadet graduates have scant respect for certain officers. I do not blame them. We are not competent. No one could become competent in two months. I discovered that they do not approve of some of the things we learned at Leavenworth—certain little exceptions to the methods used. Life here is going to be just as busy as it was at Ft. Leavenworth. Drill five to six hours every day, reveille at 6:30 A.M., retreat 5:45 P.M.—Officers meeting at 6 P.M. and officers school from 7:00 P.M. to 9:00. After taking out mess (chow) periods there is not much left of the day..

January 1, 1918

The barracks are all woefully overcrowded. Cots are jammed up close together and the influenza and pneumonia epidemic is bound to spread. Further, the quarantine people use the same mess hall that we do, they merely go at a different hour.

January 17, 1918

Letter from Hoboken, N. J., prior to overseas shipment. The train was full of soldiers— mostly young enlisted men. They were not the rollicking bunch that you usually see. The real meaning of the adventure is coming to them, I think. I could notice some such effect on our own bunch. Personally I do not feel any different from the way I did when I started for Leavenworth. I felt it in my bones that I would see overseas service before I was through with it. I have never made a secret of the fact that nothing short of a stern sense of duty could drag me across the Atlantic. In the words of the Irishman 'I never left anything over there to go back after.' But the necessity exists and I never could look the world in the face if I sidestepped this duty.

February 22, 1918

Remarks on trip to London; Generally unimpressed with the city, particularly its shops and stores. Officers are allowed to associate with the nurses, YWCA workers and anoth-

er bunch that works in the canteens but are not allowed to have anything to do with the Woman's Auxiliary Army Corps known as the W.A.A.C's (Wacs). They seem to be the enlisted men's perquisite. From what I have seen of them this is no great hardship for the officers.

February 24, 1918

Is it not most disgusting the plight the Russian revolution has put Russia into? It is unfortunate that the Grand Duke Nicholas could not have a free hand in handling things just now. Of course Lenin, Trotsky, et al would see the whole country overrun before they would consent to anything like this.

March 18, 1918

French women are certainly born with an innate love of flirting. The way they coyly cast a glance (at some of the younger officers) and then allow their lashes to immediately fall is quite fetching I would imagine, for one who was not quite so old. We hear even less from the front than you do in the States.

March 20, 1918

I saw a scene on the street this week that was the limit. Two men and a woman were walking along the street. They stopped and calmly urinated against the wall and conversed with the woman while doing so. The woman was not at all jarred. Our post urinal is out in the open and in plain view of some of the walks.

One of the officers spoke of seeing a woman ele-vate her skirt and proceeded to relieve herself.

The soldiers' mail that we censor is quite a study in human nature. Some of the men put most of their effort in convincing their wives and sweethearts that they are living correctly despite their perilous surroundings. Others apparently are trying to convince the world at large that they are regular devils. I heard an officer state the predicament of rank quite aptly the other day—a commissioned officer had no chance with the girls because the enlist-ed men had grabbed them and furthermore, did not dare to venture out with a lady of the evening because General John J. Pershing had issued a general order for summary court mar-tial for any officer seen on the street or in the company with a woman of ill fame...as far as my personal observation goes there are not nearly as many professionals on the street here as there were in London. Of course this is a much smaller town. I am led to believe that cleanli-ness is not a prime virtue of the French. Many of the people one sees on the street look like they were not very clean. Nearly all the men in their letters speak of the French being friendly but state that they cannot understand the French character. One of the officers spoke of meeting some Frenchman who kissed him on one cheek and wanted to kiss the other but was not permitted.

May 5, 1918

It is astonishing that the French as a rule have no racial antipathy toward Chinese or

Niggers. Tales are current about camp of certain Chinks and Niggers leaving camp to spend the night with French women. Granted that these women are not of the highest class the fact remains that they are selecting an off color lover when there is no doubt that there are white men available in sufficient numbers to satisfy the local demand. I have noticed Chinese in the store in Chebrais—they are apparently on terms of easy intimacy with the sales people—nearly always women.

June 9, 1918

We are forbidden to flog the Chinese. I believe that this is a mistake. It is the only corrective they know and this is no time to teach them the rule of kindness scheme. I am not reverting to barbarism but while we are compelling our citizens to go out and get shot up why should we hesitate to compel our allies to go out and earn more money than they ever earned in their lives for doing a half day's work? When the Chinese were first brought here some people kidded themselves into believing that the Chinese sense of fair play was sufficient to secure results from the money paid them, but this is a matter of driving them from morning until night.

June 12, 1918

We have some tough birds in this company. Some were rebels in the Boxer War of 1900 in China. One man chopped two others with an ax in their beds a month ago in another company.

The French imprisoned him 15 days and transferred him to my company. I tried for six weeks to arrive at terms of understanding with these Chinks but it cannot be done. For the past two weeks I have simply driven them and things go much better. No strikes, far less malingering, less trouble in the squads and the men have more respect for me and for the squad leaders. Incidently I feel much surer of my ability to set them out at the appointed time in this way.

July 14, 1918

Remarks on Chinese laborers' strike: Chinks would not work. It seems that they think that they have been worked too hard. The interpreter states that they were driven from morning until night. I admit the charge. In this respect I felt grateful to know that the Chinks had felt the pressure. At the rate they work under pressure it leads one to wonder what they would do if this pressure was removed.

August 25, 1918

I now have a detail of 70 Niggers digging on the waterworks project.

September 15, 1918

German prisoners draw exactly the same rations here that American soldiers do—have the same number and the same kind of blankets, the same underwear and the same clothes except they are dyed black. I imagine that it is the softest thing the Huns have encountered recently..

The South State and 35th Street streetcar lines were considered "Nigger" Lines by some white folks because of the large number of Negroes who rode them.

September 30, 1918

> *George was much disgusted that I seemed to be burying my talents driving Chinks. I was disgusted myself. I am yet. But that is the way things are done here. No one is working up to capacity. It is a rotten system and apparently no one dares to change it.*

November 17, 1918

> *The Paris edition of the Tribune is running a column devoted to the relative merits of French vs American girls and letters are requested from soldiers. It certainly is slush. It*

looks like all the ___ (sic) fools in the American army are trying to break into print.

In considering the location on Marquette Road (6700 South) three (3) blocks from State—do you realize that one going on any streetcar north from that locality would have to ride in a car jammed with Niggers? Before taking definite action better try some of the streetcars from that vicinity and see if this is not true. If I were still at the Amalgamated plant I would have to ride State and 35th lines. Both are Nigger lines. Cottage Grove would be pretty near as bad.

December 7, 1918

One thing that does stir me up just at present is the fact that I am asked to work my detail today while Captain Morris and his bunch of Kikes are off duty... Captain Morris is 26 years old. His qualification card shows that he is an expert in half a dozen lines yet he has fallen down on every job he has been assigned to over here. On one job he was relieved and his 2nd Lieutenant succeeded him. His company is composed of Jews.

January 14, 1919

I am working with a Nigger outfit today. It will surprise you when I tell you that they are as good a lot of workers as I have ever encountered. Their noncoms are White. That may be the solution. The noncoms do not fraternize with the men and hence have no compunction about pushing them.

January 21, 1919

We acquired a Catholic Chaplain some few days ago with a cavalry squadron. He is a typical Irishman and immediately on arrival started a scheme by which he would acquire private quarters for himself. It did not work.

June 19, 1919

The final issue of The Stars and Stripes came out today. It looks to me like the buck privates on the staff took the opportunity to air their resentment toward the officers and the army system in general.

hicagoans jam the intersection of State and Madison Streets on Armistice Day, November , 1918, to celebrate the end of the great war.

A welcome home kiss from a stranger.

Attorney Robert S. Abbott, publisher and founder of the Chicago Defender. His paper was distributed throughout the South where it sparked the northern migration during World War I and beyond.

Chapter IV

The Nineteen Twenties Roared Like A Lion For The White Vets And A Kitten For The Blacks

The returning war veterans of the Eighth Regiment did not find the world as envisioned by F. Scott Fitzgerald in "The Great Gatsby" instead, they saw planet earth as seen through the eyes of Black visionaries such as Richard Wright in his classic novel "Native Son" and in Langston Hughes' poem "Prayer For A Winter Night" or Ralph Ellison's monumental novel "Invisible Man."

The Ku Klux Klansmen were in charge in the 1920s and beyond as evidenced by their 1925 40,000 man parade down Pennsylvania Avenue in Washington, D. C. where they passed and gave faces right at the White House.

In 1921, Whites living in the shadow of the University of Chicago found a demand by other Whites for both apartments and homes in the Kenwood-Hyde Park area. Thus, the Kenwood-Hyde Park Owners Association launched a vigorous campaign to move more than 1,000 Black families out of the area between 39th and 55th Streets and from Lake Park Avenue to Cottage Grove Avenue. The plan was to turn back the calendar for Colored families and shove them back to the defined "Black Belt" area north of 39th Street and west of Cottage Grove Avenue. Many overt methods were used to get rid of them short of physical violence. The acts were far from being subtle. Blacks knew that their patronage was both unwelcome and unwanted in both the grocery and drug stores, or meat markets as well as in places of amusement such as speakeasies and theaters.

Blacks were harassed and frequently arrested by the Chicago police for simply walking down any street east of Cottage Grove unless they could show proof of employment in the area. In 1927 the author

Colonel Franklin A. Denison a soldier who made the difference.

and his cousin Frank Hunter were refused admission to see Douglas Fairbanks in the movie "The Three Musketeers," written by Alexandre Dumas, a Black French writer. The movie was being shown at the Oakland Square Theater located at 39th and Drexel Boulevard one block east of Cottage Grove.

The Holy Angels Roman Catholic Church was located on Oakwood Boulevard down the street and west of the theater. Blacks were restricted to six back row pews on the west side of the church.

Waking up Black in Chicago was always a continuation of the previous night's bad dreams for most Blacks. In spite of the nightmares, there were those who saw a new world coming in the Bronzeville area. Among the keepers of the dream were visionaries such as:

Colonel Franklin A. Denison who distinguished himself as an officer in the United States Army, practiced law in Chicago after the war, and was appointed Assistant Attorney General of the State of Illinois by Governor Len Small. In 1924 Robert S. Abbott, Publisher of the Chicago Defender persuaded Senator Medill McCormick of the Chicago Tribune family to intercede with President Calvin Coolidge in securing for Colonel Denison an appointment as a member of the Mexican Claims Commission. The Colonel died in 1925. Abbott married Denison's widow Edna Rose in 1934.

Another World War I comrade who made a name for himself was former Army First Lieutenant Earl B. Dickerson who received his Doctor of Juris Prudence from the University of Chicago in 1920 in just under two years after being discharged from the Army. Dickerson was admitted to the Illinois Bar in the same year.

Louis B. Anderson arrived on the Chicago scene from Washington, D.C. Brooks Brothers sharp to work at the World Columbian Exposition in 1892.

Prior to Dickerson becoming an alderman of the 2nd Ward, in 1939 Mayor Anton Cermak had persuaded Attorney General Otto Kerner to appoint him as an Assistant Attorney General where he served from 1932 until 1939. He served in the post until he resigned to take his seat in the Council chambers. He was so highly thought of he was permitted by the political establishment to appoint his friend Attorney Loring B. Moore as his successor. He served as a member of

Mayor William E. Dever (third from the left), appoints Attorney Earl B. Dickerson (second from the right), to the position of Assistant Corporation Counsel in 1923.

the Chicago City Council from 1939 to 1943.

During the entire period from 1921 to 1955 he also served as General Counsel for the Supreme Liberty Life Insurance Company the largest Negro owned insurance company in the North. In 1955 he was elected President of the Supreme Liberty Life Insurance Company. Early in his tenure with Supreme Life in 1923 he was invited by Mayor William E. Dever and appointed as Assistant Corporation Counsel.

Dickerson was extremely active in the Civil Rights Movement throughout his entire life. He worked with such men as Paul Robeson, A. Philip Randolph, Dr. W.E.B. DuBois, Dr. Martin Luther King, Attorney Thurgood Marshall and many other individuals who were involved in the struggle for liberation.

Another member of the Eighth Infantry Illinois National Guard was Louis B. Anderson.

Anderson was born on April 17, 1870 in Petersburg, Virginia. He was a graduate of Virginia State College in Ettrick. He came to Chicago in 1892 and worked as secretary to Major Moses P. Handy, Promoter General of the World Columbian Exposition, commonly known as the Chicago World Exposition. When the World's Fair closed in 1893 he went with Buffalo Bill as secretary.

While in the Eighth Infantry Anderson held the rank of Captain and Regimental Adjutant under Colonel Franklin A. Denison. In 1916 he remained in Chicago to recruit after the regiment was sent to Texas for active duty in the Mexican border clashes. In 1919 he was elected Alderman of the 2nd Ward and also the second Black to serve in the Chicago City Council where he served for seven consecutive terms. He was the Chairman of the Finance Committee during Mayor Dever's term. He succeeded Oscar DePriest who was not reelected because he was accused of closing his eyes to illicit activities in the 2nd Ward.

Anderson became friends with Robert S. Abbott when they were both students and subsequently graduated with honors from Chicago Kent College of Law. When Mr. Abbott founded the Chicago Defender in May, 1905 while seated at the kitchen table of Mrs. Henrietta Moore's home at 3159 South State Street, Mr. Anderson was there and became one of Mr. Abbott's founding contributing editors.

One of the most powerful Black politicians in America for a period of 30 years was also a product of World War I. He was First Lieutenant William L. Dawson who served in France with Lieutenant Earl B. Dickerson, Lieutenant Oscar Brown, Colonel Franklin Denison and Lieutenant Binga Desmond.

Dawson was born in Albany, Georgia on April 26, 1886. He graduated Magna Cum Laude from Fisk University in 1909. He studied Law at Chicago Kent College of Law and Northwestern University Law School. He was admitted to the Illinois Bar in 1920.

He was the first Black congressman to chair a major Congressional Committee (House Committee on Government

Congressman William L. Dawson and President Harry S. Truman exchanging World War I experiences.

Operation). From 1942 to his death on November 9, 1970 he was reelected from the predominantly Black wards on the southside of Chicago. He also served as Chairman for the Democratic National Committee.

Dawson in his maiden speech before the house spoke in defense Dr. William (Dean) Pickens a staff member of the U.S. Treasury Department. He said:

> *Mr. Chairman, it is with the greatest measure of hesitation that I, a new member, rise to address this august body at this time. I am sustained only by the knowledge that I can bring to this committee an understanding of the background of this subject matter better than*

Dr. William (Dean) Pickens, a staff member of the U.S. Treasury Department.

any other person in this assembly.

I have known William Pickens for more than forty years. I know his activities among my people and when I say "my people," I am not one who is sensitive to color. I am not one who is ashamed of what God made me. I stand before you further sustained by the knowledge that no man can question the loyalty of William L. Dawson to the United States of America. During the last war, although I was above draft age and did not have to go, yet, believing it was the duty of every citizen to rally to the colors in time of danger, I volunteered, was commissioned a First Lieutenant of Infantry and led Black Americans into battle. I saw them fight, and I saw them die for this flag and country of ours. And if the years had not shattered this old frame of mine and if an accident had not maimed me, instead of standing in Congress of the United States, I would today, if I had my way, be back once again defending the flag, the only flag we know.

William Pickens has been charged with being a Communist. The gentleman who recited the great organizations that he belongs to, and so forth referred to 1927. I wish I could command words well enough to convey to you something of the psychology of an underprivileged people, something of the psychology of a people who are told they have every right in fact, but who know they do not have those rights in actuality. I wish you could envision in your own minds how we struggle wherever we can to make the Constitution and our democracy a living reality. I know something about communism; I know how the Communists have tried to infiltrate among our people, playing upon the ills we have suffered and so forth. And I know how often they did not come to us under the name of Communist but came with loud-sounding names, talking of freedom, talking of democracy, and talking of inalienable rights, things that are dear to the heart of every American, be he white or be he Black. At some time or other, the names of many of us have been found connected with some of these organizations before we knew their true complexion because the more prominent the individuals were, the more insidious was their approach. I am telling you things you know.

You refer to 1927. That is a long time ago. Many names might be found on the rolls of some organization that has since been deemed a *subversive organization. I say to you, William Pickens is not a Communist and has never been a Communist. William Pickens has not knowingly affiliated himself with a Communist organization, knowing it was Communist.*

Certainly, he might have spoken at communistic meetings. I have done the same thing; in fact, I do not fear Communists. I do not fear them. I fight them, and I know that is the only way we can hold to our ideals. We have not yielded to them in their effort to infiltrate our group; and certainly, I know the voice of William Pickens has always been heard in defense of the high ideals of this country.

I say to you, Mr. Chairman, that his name has been used, but I know of my own knowledge that when he found it out, he sent in his resignation. This has been done by many loyal Americans, white and Black, who went into the thing for an ideal only to find that the thing had been organized for another purpose.

Mr. Chairman, this thing is far-reaching in its effects. I know this Congress will not condemn any man because of his race, and I am not standing here pleading for that reason, because I have been the American sense of fair play demonstrated on many an occasion. The only hope Black America has is the fundamental ideal of fair play that we know rests deep down in the bosom of the majority of the American public.

So, I am not saying that this thing is done on account of color, but I am saying to you that those who make the charge are not in a position to know of their own knowledge whereof they speak.

I do not know who their agents are. I know

William Pickens was never called before the committee and given an opportunity to answer any charge against him.

I do not know who their agents are, but let me tell you their agents do not know William Pickens like we know him. They only know what might be seen in a list of a certain number of organizations.

But we know William Pickens in the flesh. We know that William Pickens has been the means of going up and down the length and breadth of this country teaching Americanism.

I tell you of my own knowledge, and from my knowledge of doing work among my own group, that he was deserted by a certain crowd that was insistent on certain demands, and William Pickens demanded that the government be placed first.

He was for the preservation of America above all domestic problems, and for that reason he was deserted by many of those who at one time had been associated with him.

He has been the means of millions of dollars of our money going into war bonds. One insurance company alone has bought over a million dollars worth of bonds. Others have bought up to the limit and will buy more. The rank and file of us are going down in our pockets to buy.

We do not care what the organizations may be I may say to the gentleman from Texas, but this we do know that William Pickens has never been a Communist.

William Pickens is a true American, and I state that with all the integrity of a man who would fight and die for America today.

When Dawson finished his maiden speech, the members of the House lifted the roof with thunderous applause and cheers. The first person to shake Dawson's hand and congratulate him after he had completed his address was Representative Hatton W. Sumners of Texas, chairman of the House Judiciary Committee.

The stock market crash on Wall Street October 24, 1929 ignited the Great Depression.

Chapter V

The Depression Years Following The "Don't Give A Damn" Roaring 20s

Following the stock market crash on October 24, 1929, a minimum of 659 banking institutions went out of business. That number of bank failures was doubled in 1930 by an additional 1,350 closings. In 1931, 2,293 more banks shut their doors permanently, and another 1,453 followed in their footsteps in 1932.

Historically, banks and businesses have always walked in lock step thus many firms went down the tube with their bankrupt sponsors and took the life savings of hundreds of thousands of stockholders with them. The President of the Union Cigar Company could not face his board of directors and stockholders or the idea of being poor again, therefore, he opted to jump to his death from the ledge of his hotel room window when his company's stock fell from $113.50 a share to only $4.00 in a single day. Up until the 1930s our financial institutions were largely unregulated. As the stock went down, the suicide rate went up, 13.9 deaths for every 100,000 people in 1929 to 15.6 in 1930.

In an attempt to stop the suicidal madness at the epoch of the Depression, President Herbert C. Hoover promised the populace two chickens in every pot and a car in every garage. Days later from the Oval Office in the White House the President stated while holding a Havana, Cuba cigar in his left hand that economic recovery was indeed just around the corner.

In Chicago at the time of his economic pronouncements, at least 100,000 Blacks out of a population of 233,903 were receiving

President Herbert Hoover on more than one occasion said: "Prosperity is just around the corner". The rich got richer and the poor people got deeper in debt.

some form of private welfare assistance. Hence, they had reasons to wonder at what time and on what corner the President was talking about because their economic needs were life threatening and without charity they could not afford 10 cents for a quart of milk, 29 cents for a dozen eggs, 5 cents for a 20 ounce loaf of bread or 7 cents for transportation to the stockyards or steel mills in an effort to find employment as menial laborers. The President vetoed a 2 billion dollar relief bill and said: *"Our country has not become great because of political logrolling."*

The search for employment sent World War I veterans along with several million civilian men, women and children from the general population crisscrossing the country as stowaways in railroad boxcars. The freight train police ignored the "Hoover's Hobos" because there was not enough room in the jailhouses to hold them.

Father Divine and other religious groups were offering low price meals and free ones to those who were absolutely destitute.

The typical unemployment line in every city in America during the 1930s. During this period, Eddie Cantor was singing: "Now's the Time to Fall in Love, Because Potatoes and Tomatoes are Cheaper".

The terrible Thirties depicted by the world renown Playboy Magazine artist, Buck Brown.

Hobos were collectively peeping around every corner in the 48 states hoping that they would find the prosperity that President Hoover said they could expect. Economic misery invaded every region of the country, every ethnic group and every occupation from porters to presidents. Black folks had always been the last to be hired when the economic times were good and first to be fired when times were bad.

The wealthiest nation in the world learned that being really poor was spelled according to the late Blues singer Joe Williams, with four O's as opposed to two. Millions of people went from being home-

White comics in "Black-Voice". Freeman Gosden, left played "Amos" to Charles Correll's "Andy" on the radio for several decades. Both men became multi million-ires caricaturing Negroes.

owners to room renters. In the first six months of 1931 the Cook County Bailiff's office in Chicago evicted approximately 1400 families. The Chicago Urban League reported on August 25, 1931 that every available dry spot of ground and every bench on the Negro side of Washington Park between 51st and 61st Street east of South Parkway (King Drive) was covered with sleepers. In the winter, men would wrap themselves in newspapers (they were called *"Hoover blankets"*), and sleep in hallways and under stairways. The radio comics, Amos and Andy summed up the hopelessness of the period and the people with a grim story of a man who went to a hotel and asked for a room and the clerk inquired, "For sleeping or jumping?"

In Chicago the unemployed marched on City Hall. Chicago schoolteachers protesting drastic budget cuts pulled down the 1933 World's Fair Flag and stormed City Hall. From March, 1930, to September, 1934 there were eight paydays on time for school employees and seven payless paydays in the four year period were in script,

The Century of Progress Exposition where Sally Rand gained fame as a fan dancer was held on Chicago's lakefront between 12th and 39th Streets in the Spring and Summer of 1933 and 1934.

not cash. At midmorning May 10, 1930, a 25 year old woman leaped to her death from the 10th floor of the building at 36 South State Street, because she had lost her job at a mail order company six months earlier, and had not been able to find another.

The first warlike confrontation between the WWI veterans and the White House shook an already trembling Washington, D. C. in the summer of 1932. Congress was considering a bill authorizing immediate issuance of bonuses already allotted to First World War Veterans, but not due for payment until 1945. To lobby for the bill, fifteen thousand unemployed veterans and their families converged on the nation's capitol, calling themselves the Bonus Expeditionary Force (BEF). They camped in crude shacks and tents on vacant lots, parks and in empty government buildings. Black folks mingled with the whites. "Jim Crow was Absent Without Leave," said Roy Wilkins of the National Association for the Advancement of Colored People (NAACP).

President Hoover opposed the bonus bill, the House of Representatives passed it. The Senate voted it down after a great deal of debating. Following the Senate's action a leader of the BEF shouted: "We were heroes in 1917, but we are bums today." Many of the bonus marchers vacated Washington, but several thousand lingered behind in their tent and shack cities. It is unfortunate that President Hoover lost his composure, and impulsively labeled the war veterans "insurrectionists and communists" and refused to meet with them.

Annual Earnings: 1932 to 1934	
AIRLINE PILOT	$8,000.00
AIRLINE STEWARDESS	$1,500.00
APARTMENT HOUSE SUPERINTENDENT	$1,500.00
BITUMINOUS COAL MINER	$723.00
BUS DRIVER	$1,373.00
CHAUFFEUR	$624.00
CIVIL SERVICE EMPLOYEE	$1,284.00
COLLEGE TEACHER	$3,111.00
CONSTRUCTION WORKER	$907.00
DENTIST	$2,391.00
DEPARTMENT STORE MODEL	$936.00
DOCTOR	$3,382.00
DRESSMAKER	$780.00
ELECTRICAL WORKER	$1,559.00
ENGINEER	$2,520.00
FIRE CHIEF (city of 30,000 to 50,000)	$2,075.00
HIRED FARM HAND	$216.00
HOUSEMOTHER—BOYS' SCHOOL	$780.00
LAWYER	$4,218.00
LIVE-IN MAID	$260.00
MAYOR (city of 30,000 to 50,000)	$2,317.00
PHARMACEUTICAL SALESMAN	$1,500.00
POLICE CHIEF (city of 30,000 to 50,000)	$2,636.00
PRIEST	$831.00
PUBLIC SCHOOL TEACHER	$1,227.00
PUBLICITY AGENT	$1,800.00
RAILROAD EXECUTIVE	$5,064.00
RAILROAD CONDUCTOR	$2,729.00
REGISTERED NURSE	$936.00
SECRETARY	$1,040.00
STATISTICIAN	$1,820.00
STEELWORKER	$422.87
STENOGRAPHER-BOOKKEEPER	$936.00
TEXTILE WORKER	$435.00
TYPIST	$624.00
UNITED STATES CONGRESSMAN	$8,663.00
WAITRESS	$520.00

The salary scale for those who were lucky enough to be employed in 1932 to 1934.

In July 1932 with Hoover's blessings General Douglas McArthur, assisted by Majors Dwight D. Eisenhower and George S. Patton confronted the veterans and their families with a horse cavalry, tanks and soldiers at the ready with rifles equipped with bayonets. Several irritated members of the BEF hurled stones and bricks at the mounted cavalry. The scene that followed horrified the nation. Men

President Franklin D. Roosevelt shown delivering his maiden "Fireside Chat" from the White House on Sunday evening March 12, 1933. Wherever President Roosevelt appeared the band would strike up: "Happy Days Are Here Again".

and women were chased and trampled down by the horsemen; little children were teargassed; the shacks and tents were set afire. As the smoke floated above Walter Reed Veterans' Hospital and the capitol's stately buildings, a United Press correspondent said the following about the ugly spectacle, "*so all the misery and sufferings had finally come to this; United States soldiers marching with loaded guns against fellow American citizens.*" The answer to the predicament that Hoover created was not violence but food and drink.

When Presidential hopeful Franklin D. Roosevelt heard about the government's violent attack on the Bonus Army he turned to his

The National Recovery Act almost missed Black professionals, in that many Black doctors, dentists, lawyers, and teachers were employed full time holding skin and bones together with low paying jobs as Postal clerks and Pullman porters during the entire Depression and beyond.

advisor Felix Frankfurter and said: *"Well, Felix, this will elect me."* (Frankfurter was appointed by President Roosevelt as an Associate Supreme Court Justice in 1939.)

President Hoover's insensitive attitude toward the Bonus

A sleeping car porter with Bachelor and Master degrees in Engineering from the Massachusetts Institute of Technology watches a white executive step up to his Pullman car berth.

Army mirrored his negative attitude about Negroes generally. Blacks were aware that the President shared the prevailing white feeling about Negroes. The establishment Blacks knew that Hoover was attempting to push them out of the Republican Party in an effort to attract Southern Democrats.

Hoover wanted a lily-white Grand Old Party. He had disbanded the Negro division of the Republican National Committee, rejected appeals for an anti-lynching law, and continued the segregation of the army and the use of Jim Crow eating and toilet facilities in Federal buildings in the nation's capitol. Hoover's philosophy of individualism, opportunity and fair play for Negroes was spelled out on the signs posted across America that read: "For Whites Only."

During this very depressed period, Hollywood and Tin Pan Alley attempted to lift the spirit of the people with songs like: *On the Sunny Side of the Street; Cheerful Little Earful, Stardust; Mood Indigo; Moonglow,* and Duke Ellington's *Sophisticated Lady.*

When President Franklin D. Roosevelt took office on March 4, 1933 he carried with him two presidential proclamations, one summoning a special session of Congress, the other declaring a National Bank Holiday, suspending banking transactions throughout the nation. The time had come for Roosevelt and his administration to roll up their sleeves and go to work producing the New Deal the President had promised the American people.

The first measure, the Emergency Banking Relief Bill, was introduced just before 1P.M. On March 9, 1933 it passed sight unseen by a unanimous House vote, it was approved 73 to 7 in the Senate, and signed into Law by the President at 8:36 P.M. that evening. The act provided for the reopening of the banks under Treasury Department license applicable to banks that were solvent and the reorganization and management of those that were not. The bill also gave the President broad powers over credit, currency, and the buying and selling of gold and silver.

On Sunday evening March 12, 1933 President Franklin D. Roosevelt broadcast the first of his many *"Fireside Chats"* and 60 million people heard his mellow voice booming with confidence on their radios. His message: *Banks are once again a safe place to deposit your savings.*

Early the following Monday morning in lieu of people being poised for a run on the banks to withdraw their monies out of the savings institutions and hide it in the mattress they were waiting patiently to deposit or redeposit their hard earned funds. With the stroke of his pen and the ability to articulate the thought that we have nothing to fear but fear itself, Roosevelt was on the road to restoring confidence in capitalism.

The President's next move was to pump the economy with his

Over 200,000 plus African-Americans, unlike this clerk at a camp head-quarters in Illinois, served in the Civilian Conservation Corps as grunts.

alphabet soup programs such as the Civil Conservation Corps (CCC); which provided direct cash grants to the states to operate camps that would eventually accommodate 2.5 million young men between the ages of eighteen and twenty-five. They would work at planting trees, building bridges, dams, reservoirs, fish ponds and fire towers.

The Colored CCC boys served in segregated companies the same as their fathers had in World War I. Over 200,000 Negroes enrolled in the program between 1933 and 1942. They were paid a dollar a day plus three Hots and a Flop. Twenty-five dollars of the thirty they earned was mailed by the government directly to their Depression stricken families back home.

On June 16, 1933 he established the Public Works program (PWA) for older men with families, it was funded with a fund of $3.3 billion to build roads, sewage and water systems, public buildings and a sundry of other projects. The jobs paid $55.00 per month.

he USS Arizona was one of the more seriously damaged United States ships at Pearl Harbor on December 7, 1941. Many of the more than 2,000 officers and enlisted men illed at Pearl Harbor were buried alive in ships like the Arizona.

The Tennessee Valley Authority (TVA) was followed by the National Industrial Recovery Act (NIRA). The passage of the NIRA, called for an industry wide code establishing minimum wage and maximum hours. The Congress adjourned on June 16, 1932 with its first One Hundred Days completed under the new President. President Roosevelt had delivered fifteen messages to Congress during that 100 day period and fifteen significant laws had been enacted.

In less than a decade after President Franklin Delano Roosevelt took office, America was in the midst of World War II.

World War II

Captain David W. Pelkey

Chapter VI

A Pre World War II 184th Regiment Volunteer

David W. Pelkey received his Master's Degree in Political Science from the University of Illinois at Champaign-Urbana in June 1940. His initial plan was to return to school in the Fall of 1940 and enroll in a two-year accelerated doctorate program. After a family meeting it was decided that he would volunteer for a one year hitch in the Army since he was a prime candidate for the draft. He had been classified by his draft board as 1-A under the new Selective Service Act.

On November 6, 1940, Pelkey joined the 184th Field Artillery National Guard and was shipped to Fort Custer, Michigan on January 5, 1941 when the 184th was activated into active duty. Captain John Harris promoted Private Pelkey to Machine Gun Sergeant twenty-five days after the regiment reached Fort Custer on January 6.

In the Fall of 1940 the agenda being articulated by General George C. Marshall, U.S. Chief of Staff, was to give all National Guard Units one year of active service. However, subliminally everybody knew from the uncontrollable growling in their large gut that America was preparing to go to war following the Germans invasion of Poland in September 1939. The officers and men of the 184th Regiment never made the upcoming war a part of any discussion. In August of 1941 the United States Chief of Staff extended the original twelve month active duty calendar for the National Guard to eighteen months. Four months later, on Sunday, December 7, 1941, the United States was attacked by Japanese Zeros diving out of the heavens, dropping bombs on the land and the ships in the harbor of the island of Pearl Harbor, Hawaii. Active military service following this major disaster was automatically extended for the duration of the war plus six months.

The mind-set of knowing that the Army was going to be your home for an indefinite period of time was not one to relish with glee unless you were a "jack in the box" career soldier. If you were not 4F (physically unfit) the option of not serving in the Armed Forces was to be absent without leave (AWOL) and going over the hill.

Fort Custer had its Colored neighborhood the same as Detroit, Michigan and Chicago, Illinois. The Colored troops and officers were housed in the "Black Belt" pocket of the camp area, the same as they were in the cities. There was no escape from being Colored, not even on paper. If a bulletin, general order, or special order was issued from the third Service Command and a Colored officer's name appeared on it, beside his name would be an asterisk, i.e., Major John Doe*. This was a code message to the white military world that you were not one of their kind.

Within the 184th Field Artillery you did not have to worry about being their kind to rise in the ranks because everybody was Colored from the foot soldier to the colonel. Promotions were not based on race; your ability to perform was usually the barometer for moving up in rank. David Pelkey's performance was superior in that he was promoted from Sergeant to Second Lieutenant and Munitions Officer in the field while on maneuvers in Arkansas. His notice of the promotion to Lieutenant was received in a telegram dated September 15, 1941 to Lieutenant Colonel Marcus H. Ray, the Battalion Commander, from Colonel Anderson F. Pitts, the Regimental Commanding Officer.

An interesting sidelight to Pelkey's field promotion was that he had not been in the service twelve months and was not considered officer material by his immediate superior. Those who were anointed to be leaders in the 184th Field Artillery were given green bands to wear around the biceps of their left arms. Pelkey was serious, smart and low key. He was not a "lipstick wearer" or the kind of person who would make any effort to draw attention to himself.

For reasons unknown to David Pelkey he was never scheduled to take the Army's intelligence aptitude test, nor did he every apply or go to Officers Candidate School. He told the author, who had known

Captain Edward D. Wimp, Jr. a member of the 184th and his wife Elizabeth at 12th Street train station shortly before the Captain boarded the train for Camp Custer, Michigan on January 5, 1941.

him for over fifty years, that at the time of this interview he thought that the reason he was considered for a field commission was because it was suspected by somebody on high that there was an outside possibility that he might have some sense. A year after he was made 2nd Lieutenant in the field he was promoted to 1st Lieutenant and Assistant Battery Executive under Captain E. Johnson. In November 1942 he became Commander of Headquarters Battery under Colonel Anderson Pitts.

In reference to his series of elevations David Pelkey said: "I worked hard on every assignment I was given. I would say that they did not give me anything but a chance. A chance for me was an opportunity to do the job. I was mentally and physically prepared to take advantage of the opportunity."

On January 17, 1943 the 184th Field Artillery was split up as a regiment at Fort Custer, Michigan. Some of the men were shipped to Camp Butner, North Carolina, under the command of Lieutenant

Colonel Wendell T. Derrick of the 930th Field Artillery Battalion. David Pelkey and the other segment of the former regiment became the 931st Field Artillery under the command of Lieutenant Colonel Marcus Ray and were sent to Camp Forrest, Tennessee. It was in Tennessee that they were pulled out of the theater at gunpoint. (This incident is described by 1st Lieutenant Earl Strayhorn in detail in Chapter VII.)

Following the theater incident the 931st Field Artillery was sent to Camp Gordon, Georgia on April 28, 1943. It was in Camp Gordon that the enlisted men and all officers were separated. The enlisted men were sent to the Quartermasters and the officers were sent to the 92nd Division in Fort Huachuca, Arizona. The 92nd Division troops were Colored and most of the officers were white, except for a handful of 2nd Lieutenants. The Negro officers from Camp Gordon replaced most of the white officers who were commanding Colored troops.

Pelkey had been in command of a Field Artillery battery in Camp Custer, Michigan, Camp Forrest, Tennessee and Camp Gordon, Georgia. When he took over Battery A of the 600 Field Artillery Battalion at Fort Huachuca he used the same Colored artillery officers that had been with him in the three aforementioned camps.

The men and officers of the 600 Field Artillery spent about one month getting their act together at Huachuca before they headed for Camp Patrick Henry, Virginia, a port of embarkation, on April 14, 1944. When they reached the port in Virginia, Pelkey discovered that they had room on the ship for all the field artillery batteries except his. Like the late singer Otis Redding, he was left standing on the dock waiting for another ship to come in. Pelkey's Battery had to wait approximately a week before they were put on a ship. It was a French Luxury Liner converted into a troop steamer. Most of the troops on the ship were white Brazilians. This was the first time that Pelkey had witnessed white and Colored Brazilians acting as if they were all the same complexion.

Since the ship was a luxury liner it was not part of a convoy like the ones that the 92nd Division had sailed on. Convoys move slowly. The convoy left a week before the luxury steamer arrived in Camp

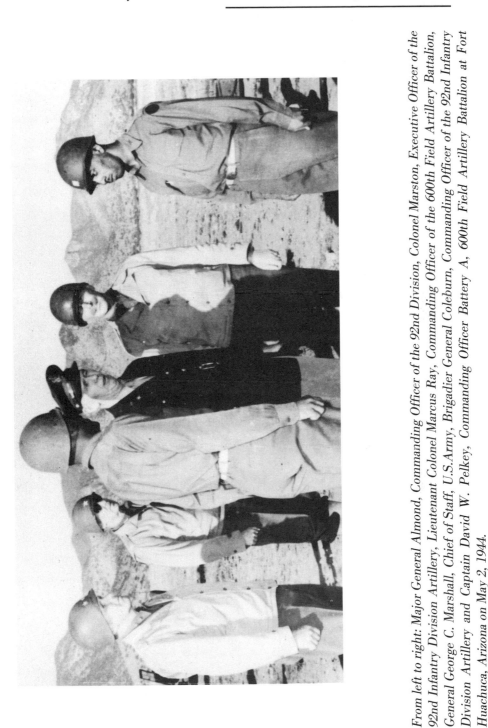

From left to right: Major General Almond, Commanding Officer of the 92nd Division, Colonel Marston, Executive Officer of the 92nd Infantry Division Artillery, Lieutenant Colonel Marcus Ray, Commanding Officer of the 600th Field Artillery Battalion, General George C. Marshall, Chief of Staff, U.S.Army, Brigadier General Coleburn, Commanding Officer of the 92nd Infantry Division Artillery and Captain David W. Pelkey, Commanding Officer Battery A, 600th Field Artillery Battalion at Fort Huachuca, Arizona on May 2, 1944.

Patrick Henry, and yet Pelkey's Battery reached Italy a little better than a week before the other battalions arrived. Since Battery A had both men and guns they were put to work as a support group for the 10th Mountain Division. Battery A of the 600 Battalion had been under some heavy firepower before the other batteries arrived. Lieutenant Colonel Marcus Ray would stand around and watch the men and officers of Battery A until the shooting started. Then he would hastily remove his behind.

Captain David N. Pelkey describes an unusual combat situation:

> During a tactically static development my Battery was put in a support position less than one-half mile from the location separating the opposing enemies' ground troops. The position made it possible for us to effect interdiction and/or counter-battery fire four to five miles deep into hostile territory. At the same time, the nature of my equipment, 155mm howitzers, made the position tactically and logistically high-risk.
>
> To this, there was added a meaningful aggravating factor. Our troops occupied sea-level positions to the troops; those mountains gave the enemy an unobstructed view of the entire area occupied by our troops. Certainly, it made it possible for observers in the mountains to see and locate a muzzle blast every time one of my guns was fired.
>
> Accordingly, for the first few days, I was in that position, we fired missions only: (1) when directed by a liaison pilot in a put-put' and (2) when the smoke generator effectively generated sufficient smoke to cover our area and preclude ready detection of our muzzle blast.
>
> The day came when I was told that I had a fire mission without a smoke cover. Pelkey in

his opinion, was being told that he was a tactical 'sacrificial lamb'.

I had, as standard operating procedure, effected reconnaissance for an alternate position; and while the gun sections were firing missions under put-put' direction we cleared the position of all the essential material and equipment.

Although our muzzle blasts were clearly identified when we were firing without smoke cover, no retaliatory action was taken while the put-puts' were in the air; the pilots could have identified locations of counter-battery fire and directed our fire at those locations.

As darkness approached, and the 'put-puts' left, we dug our guns out of position, loaded our ammunition and abandoned the position with a minimum of activity and delay.

During that evening and night we could hear artillery fire landing in what I assumed was my recently abandoned position. Later I went back; the area had been devastated by hostile fire.

The war ended in Europe in May 1945. Pelkey's Division stayed in Italy until November. Pelkey gives an eye witness account of how some soldiers got rich after the war ended.

With no activity in Europe all the battalions were sent to the staging area to be sent back home or the Pacific except my battery. What they did with my battery, they sent us up to Geneva to take over security of the dock there. Why was that necessary? Because there had been this shipment of supplies, etc. These supplies and materials were enroute when the war ended. For example, ships still were coming in with field rations. The supplies had to be stored. Logistics dictated that supplies be piled up on the docks at Geneva and they had to have someone to guard them.

So they took my battery. I was responsible for security at the docks. How much stuff was there? The 10 and 1 rations were piled up two stories high and a block long. If I had not been chicken I might have made some money or gone to jail.

One day a man came to me and said 'we would like to use two of our trucks. Just let me have two trucks. I will give you $20,000 for each of the trucks.' He was saying he was going to load the trucks with supplies and take them and make some money. I am the guy who is in charge. All I had to do was say, take them and go, but I was chicken.

I know one officer who was responsible for the Post Exchange merchandise. He sold two half ton trucks of PX supplies and reported that the trucks fell over one of those cliffs.

Talking about making money. Guys would get MP armbands. Just say three of them would get MP bands and one of them would take a jeep and catch a local citizen with some money and ask him if he wanted to buy a jeep. If the answer is positive you tell him to meet you on such and such a corner. The other two partners in this triangle of greed, wearing MP armbands, would stop the guy on the next corner threaten to arrest him and take the jeep back. The three thieves end up with the jeep and the money. The number of soldiers who became rich in Europe will never be known.

After the war Pelkey graduated from law school and entered the private practice of law in Chicago, Illinois. Some years later he moved to Washington, D. C. and became an Administrative Judge for the General Services Administration where he conducted hearings and resolved disputes between government contracting personnel and firms having contracts to furnish supplies and services under contracts administered by such personnel.

In addition, he conducted hearings and resolved disputes as an Administrative Law Judge between Dept. Of Labor contracting personnel and Dept. Of Labor (DOL) contractors.

He also served as an Assistant General Counsel, Claims and Litigation Division, General Services Administration, where he supervised the activities of as many as 21 trial attorneys.

David W. Pelkey retired in February 1983. He made his final transition in 1998 in Washington, D. C. but was buried in the Oakwood Cemetery, in Chicago, beside his wife June Evans who had preceded him in death.

Judge Earl Strayhorn
Former U.S. Army 1st Lieutenant and retired Lieutenant Colonel.

Chapter VII

A Black Fly In A Bottle Of Buttermilk

arl Strayhorn was inducted into the Armed Forces on October 14, 1941 after completing a cursory physical examination at an induction station located on Van Buren near State Street in Chicago, Illinois. Following the brief swearing in ceremony he and approximately 100 other young Colored men were immediately transported on the Illinois Central Railroad to Fort Custer, in Battle Creek, Michigan for eight weeks of basic training. The basic training was aborted, without the benefit of rifle training, after three weeks because a special order came down from the Sixth Area Headquarters directing that a detachment of 45 men be transferred immediately to Tuskegee, Alabama.

Strayhorn, the acting leader in charge, and the 44 other new soldiers were greeted at Tuskegee by a cold Alabama wind. The barracks at Tuskegee had not been completed, therefore, the three week old recruits spent their first ten nights in Alabama sleeping under canvas tents equipped with wood burning stoves and some freshly cut logs that had not been aged for burning. Each morning one man in each tent had to knock the soot off of the spark deflectors in order to get a proper draft for the simmering ashes as well as prevent the sparks from igniting the untreated tent material that the Army was using at that period.

Since there were no officers on the base, Strayhorn continued to act as a leader for the 44 men. He held that leadership role until late November when a contingent of men arrived who had been in training at Chanute Field in Rantoul, Illinois specifically for the Tuskegee Experiment. The men from Chanute had not been at Tuskegee 10 days when the Japanese bombed Pearl Harbor on December 7, 1941.

Shortly after Pearl Harbor the Military Police organizational table was put in place under Commanding Officer Captain George W. Webb. The Captain appointed Earl Strayhorn as his First Sergeant, a position that he held until mid-February 1942 when he left Tuskegee to go to the Field Artillery Officers Candidate School at Fort Sills, Oklahoma.

At Fort Sills, Strayhorn was housed in a tent with five other O.C.S. candidates. "I was a fly in a bottle of buttermilk," he states. In other words, he was the only Negro in his tent. Strayhorn's tent mates were from Alabama, Texas and Brooklyn, New York. He discovered after a very brief period that the white boy from New York was more racist than the boys from the Confederate states.

There were only two Negro candidates, in addition to Strayhorn, out of a class of two hundred; all 3 graduated in the top ten percent of the class. After receiving his commission, Strayhorn was sent back to Fort Custer, Michigan where he was assigned to the 184th Field Artillery Regiment, commanded by all-Negro officers. The Regimental Commander of the 184th was Colonel Anderson F. Pitts from Chicago, Illinois. In the 27 years that Strayhorn was in the military, on active duty or in the National Guard, he never served directly under any officer who was not Negro. His experience is very unique when one considers that the philosophy of the United States Army was based on the false premise that the best leaders of Negro troops were white officers from the South.

It was the customs of the South that caused Northern colored troops numerous racial problems. An example is a race riot that came within a single gun shot of taking place at Camp Forrest, Tennessee over segregated seating in a post theater. Lieutenant Earl Strayhorn was both present and accounted for and he describes the situation as follows:

> *When we arrived at Camp Forrest, Tennessee*
> *from Camp Gordon at Augusta, Georgia, the first*
> *thing we heard was how bad Colored troops· were*
> *being treated in reference to using any facilities out-*
> *side of the designated Colored Area on the Post. All*

Regimental Commander, Colonel Anderson F. Pitts.

the Colored units, with the exception of the WACs, were insulated in one section of the camp, as if by contact they would give their white brothers in arms a severe case of 'black plague'.

On the 184th's first evening in Camp Forrest one of our First Sergeants ordered his men to line up in full Class A Uniform at 6:00 p.m. and march to the theater where they all bought tickets and took seats everywhere in the house except the area marked FOR COLORED ONLY. The commissioned Colored officers were not going to let the enlisted men outdo them, therefore they integrated the white officers' section. The white military police responded by ordering 250 Colored officers and men out of the theater at gunpoint. After they were ejected from the theater they were made to line up in a drainage ditch by the side of the road under the muzzles of sub-machine guns pointed at their heads.

One week later, the same Post Theater was showing a 4-Star picture entitled, 'This Land is Mine', which featured Charles Laughton, and included a scene of Laughton reading The Bill of Rights. A large number of officers and men wanted to see the picture so we decided we would repeat our earlier movie theater integration sit-in. This time the scene was changed because the Post Commander, Colonel M. F. Waltz, came to the theater with 50 Military Police armed with Thompson machine guns at the ready in the event things got out of control. The MPs remained outside of the theater. The Colonel had the lights turned on and he addressed First Lieutenant Robin E. L. Washington, one of our officers who was sitting on the end seat. The Colonel said: 'Lieutenant don't you see that section marked COLORED OFFICERS?' Lieutenant Washington replied: 'Yes Sir.' The Colonel then said: 'Why aren't you sitting there?' Lieutenant Washington recoiled: 'Well, Sir, when I was commissioned I did not see anything on my commission from the President of the United States designating where I should sit.' The Colonel turned beet red and blustered: 'On this Post, where there is a designation for COLORED OFFICERS, you will sit there.' Lieutenant Washington retorted: 'No, Sir! I will remain, by your leave or without your leave. I will not move out of this section marked Official Officer'. On two contiguous rows of seats, the same questions was asked and he got the same replies mouthed by Lieutenant Washington from each Negro officer, without exception.

Lieutenant Colonel Marcus H. Ray.

The Colonel, with the snap of a whip, ordered his Aide to bring in the Military Police. The MPs lined up on the left and right aisles with their Thompson Machine Guns at the ready. They had encircled the Negro officers. One of our enlisted men saw what was happening and he ran back to the Unit Area and alerted Lieutenant Colonel Marcus H. Ray about the impending crisis. Lieutenant Colonel Ray arrived in minutes after the MPs had positioned themselves and we had refused to move. The Lieutenant Colonel came down the aisle to where we were seated and said: 'Officers of the 184th follow me.' We all got up and followed our Colonel. He took us to the theater office where he met with the Post Commander, Colonel Waltz, who was a bird Colonel and out-ranked our Lieutenant

*Colonel, who wore a silver oak leaf. Colonel Waltz
said: 'Lieutenant Colonel Ray, I am going to file
charges against you for inciting a riot.' He filed
charges with the 2nd Army Commander,
Lieutenant General Lesley J. McNair. The General
neither sustained nor dismissed the charges, neither
did he convene a court martial. However, he did
relieve Colonel Waltz of his command. Waltz was
subsequently killed in the North Africa Campaign.
Today I still wonder what would have happened if
Colonel Ray had not come to the theater that night.*

The officers involved in the second theater incident were: First
Lieutenants John A. Rector, David W. Pelkey, Lawrence Langford,
Robin E. L. Washington, Welton I. Taylor, and Ernest Davenport;
Second Lieutenants Byron Minor, James Dunn, Ernest V. Williams
and Warrant Officer, Milton J. Winfield Jr.

After the first theater sit-in the 184th Field Artillery Regiment
was persona-non grata at Camp Forrest, Tennessee. They were reas-
signed to Camp Gordon, which was just a few miles outside of
Augusta, Georgia. It was at Camp Gordon that the 931st Field
Artillery Battalion, a descendant of the old 8th Illinois Infantry, was
converted into an engineer combat (hard labor) battalion.

The break up was a grim scene that brought tears from the
eyes of hardened soldiers. Lieutenant Colonel Marcus H. Ray, from
Chicago, the tall and soldierly Commander of the battalion who had
labored long hours to qualify his unit for combat duty, stood mute and
saddened as he watched the troop train leave with some of the best
men of the battalion. Some of the officers who were left standing at
the rail siding wept uncontrollably.

Captain David W. Pelkey, one of the officers left standing by
the railroad tracks, states the following:

*Since there was an unwritten rule that no
white officer could serve under a Negro superior,
the turnover at Fort Huachuca can best be under-
stood in that context. A later example took place in
1946, when the 477th, under Colonel B. O. Davis*

Jr., moved to Lockbourne Army Air Force Base in Ohio. This event marked the first time Negro officers were permitted to administer an Army Air Force Base or any other kind of military facility in the continental United States without the immediate supervision of white officers.

Strayhorn was shipped out of Fort Huachuca to a port of debarkation in Virginia with the 92nd Division in September 1944. When they landed in Naples, Italy they immediately went into the battle-line during the final days of the battle for Rome. Prior to reaching Rome the Allies and the Germans agreed that Rome was to be a free and open city and therefore would not become a part of the war. Rome was by-passed.

The 92nd Division fought in Italy until the German resistance cracked just above Florence. Up to that point the 92nd had been fighting at a disadvantage in the mountains. Out of the mountains, they poured down into the Italian farmland. The flat terrain allowed the Allies to outmaneuver the Germans with the Allies' overwhelming superior power in personnel and material.

On February 22, 1946 Strayhorn was discharged from the Army with battle ribbons and the rank of First Lieutenant. He immediately entered law school, and in 1998 retired as the presiding judge of the First Municipal District of the Circuit Court of Cook County, Illinois.

Judge Strayhorn received his undergraduate degree from the University of Illinois, Urbana, Illinois in 1941. His Juris Doctor degree was earned from DePaul University College of Law in 1948.

1st Lieutenant Robert Martin (on right) and his brother, Ensign Henry Martin.

Chapter VIII

He Rolled Out Of A Flaming P-51 Plane Over Enemy Territory

Robert Martin was born in Dubuque, Iowa, a small city that was almost one hundred percent lily-white. In 1942, there were 40,000 whites and 39 Negroes living in that tiny mid-west municipality. From 1st grade through the 12th grade he was the only person of color in his class. As a matter of fact, the city was so white that in 1990 the Mayor and the City Council placed several ads in major metropolitan newspapers inviting Negro families to come and live in "beautiful Dubuque."

The ratio of Colored students at Iowa State College in Ames mirrored Dubuque in that Martin was the only Negro student in his classrooms during the entire four years he was at the school. However, Dr. George Washington Carver, the lone Negro graduate in the Iowa State College class of 1893, had gone on to become one of the world's foremost scientists in the first half of the Twentieth Century by revolutionizing the use of the peanut and sweet potato. Dr. Carver is credited with literally saving Southern agriculture.

When Robert Martin graduated from college in June 1942 he was ripe as a Georgia peach for the Army. He was so ripe that a member of the local draft board called him via telephone and said: "Martin, if you don't report to this draft board within the next twenty-four hours we are going to send the F.B.I out there to get you." He was needed to fill the Dubuque Colored quota for September 1942.

On the other hand, Martin had a legitimate excuse for not immediately submitting himself for the draft in that he had applied for the Army Air Corps at Tuskegee and successfully passed both the written and physical examinations. He had been accepted, but not called. His explanation was not good enough for the all-white draft board. Moreover, they had never heard of the great Booker T.

Washington, of Tuskegee Institute or President Franklin D. Roosevelt's Tuskegee Experiment for Colored pilots.

In spite of Martin's protest, the local draft board sucked him in on September 24, 1942 and shipped him off to Fort Dodge, Iowa which is located just a little north of Des Moines. After settling in at Fort Dodge, Martin regurgitated his Air Corps story again to a commissioned officer. This time the commanding officer believed that there might be an ounce of truth in Martin's tale. Therefore, he verified it with the War Department and was advised by special order to hold Martin in the Reception Center until further notice.

Martin was made a member of the permanent personnel at the Reception Center. His only assignment was to work with the Supply Sergeant and pass out sheets to the thousands of recruits who came through Fort Dodge.

The local military establishment was so busy processing men and material that they did not have time to think about or practice Jim Crow. Moreover, it would have been counter productive to isolate three Colored men in a fifty bed barrack.

After six months of counting sheets at Fort Dodge, Martin was finally called to be trained as a fighter pilot at the Tuskegee Air Corps in eastern Alabama, near Montgomery. After he completed his training, he became a member of the 100th Fighter Squadron. In the meantime, the 99th Fighter Squadron was fighting in a hot war in the European Theater as an attachment to the 12th Air Force, which was flying tactical support for ground troops.

When the 100th Fighter Squadron went overseas in February 1944 it was part of the newly formed 332nd Fighter Group. The group was composed of three all-Negro squadrons: the 100th, 301st and 302nd. The group was later joined by the veteran 99th, the Alpha Squadron. The new coalition of squadrons became attached to the 15th Air Force as a support team for strategic operations. Their assignments were to escort bombers to sites where they would blow up enemy oil fields, railroads, ships and factories, etc. Having four squadrons as opposed to the ordinary three worked to the advantage of those bombers that were being protected by the 332nd Group. The Germans were less likely to attack a fighter group of four squadrons as opposed to one composed of three. Moreover, despite the fact that every pilot wanted to be an Ace, Colonel B. O. Davis Jr., Commander of the 332nd, was opposed to his pilots trying to become heroes at the cost of losing a single bomber.

The white flyers from other groups would frequently get sucked into playing Ace in the sky against the German Luftwaffe. The German pilots would taunt the American flyers by making aggressive moves and some white pilots would take off, with visions of the movie hero John Wayne in mind, to play cowboy in the sky. As soon as that gap in bomber security had been broken by the wayward pilots trying to become heroes, another group of German planes would nosedive through the clouds and blow the unprotected bomber out of the sky. The Germans rarely attacked the 332nd because they stayed together as a group dedicated to the single mission of protecting the bombers. The group established an excellent reputation because they stuck with their assignment and therefore did not lose a single bomber.

When a pilot had flown five escort bomber missions he was automatically awarded an Air Medal. The medal was sent home to his parents. On the other hand, if he was shot down and no one knew what happened to him, his parents would not receive a medal but a letter stating that their son was missing in action. Missing in action was not uncommon among pilots who went on strafing missions.

Martin was on his 64th strafing mission when his plane was shot down near Zagreb, Yugoslavia in 1945. He describes the event as follows:

> *After being hit, the engine began to smooth out, running quieter than ordinary. A few seconds later I noticed short tongues of flames coming from the exhaust stacks. The flames grew longer, but the engine continued to run smoothly. I stayed at tree-top level for perhaps a minute to get out of sight of ground observers, and the thought flashed through my mind that I would have to bailout. The flames coming from the exhaust stacks were very colorful and in the shape of long tubes, like the balloons you see at sideshows that get twisted into animals. The*

tubes of flames grew longer and longer and in seconds were encircling the bubble canopy over the cockpit.

The decision was made—you bailout or sit and become a fried charcoal Negro. I climbed to about 1000 feet above the terrain, looked out, and said to myself this is not high enough. I climbed up another 1000 feet.

To bailout, you had to disconnect the radio, oxygen, and jettison the canopy. (Some moments earlier I had sent out a Mayday call saying I was bailing out). I then rolled the plane on its back, unhooked the safety belt, and thought I was dropping free and clear. I was wrong!

I was falling out when the plane rolled over about three quarters of the way. I was falling like someone trying to run with his coattail caught in a closed door. The 300 mph wind factor was holding me attached to the plane. My body was out but my legs were still in. What to do? No debate-DO IT RIGHT. I grabbed the edge of the cockpit, pulled myself back in, sat down, grabbed the controls, leveled the plane, did a proper half roll, let go, and I was free and clear, except the tail of the plane was falling in my direction. It missed.

I counted to ten, but wait! I was the World's Greatest Fighter Pilot. This was my 64th mission, nothing could ever happen to me. I had worn my parachute straps loose so they wouldn't bind and hurt or cut off circulation during the five hour mission. However, if a chute with loose straps was opened, the force of the leg straps catching one's crotch and genitals could cause severe damage and I would be singing soprano for the rest of my life. Now, in desperation, I wound, yes, wound my legs together like a twisted rope. I pulled the rip cord,

"Queen Cole" Martin's plane.

remembering to wrap my arms around my body so I could save the rip cord to present for proof to get into the 'Caterpillar Club', the club of flyers whose lives were saved by a parachute made from the silk thread of a caterpillar cocoon.

For several seconds I was knocked out cold because when I came to, I was floating, and swinging down with a huge white parachute canopy overhead. In front of my face was the chest buckle, almost forming a new pair of goggles. I could taste blood from where the buckle had hit my chin, knocked me out cold and split my lip on the inside.

I was okay, coming down over a section of woods but with an open field nearby. Instructions were, if you pull on the shroud lines on one side, the parachute will move in that direction. Those are the

Pilots preparing for take off by strapping on parachutes..

wrong instructions. Your rate of descent will increase like you don't have a parachute. It scared me to the point I'd take a chance going into a tree and I let go of the lines. I missed the woods and landed about fifty feet away. Luckily there was little wind and I had no trouble collapsing the chute, rolling it into a ball and stuffing it under a bush. I lit out running south, away from the Germans. At mid-afternoon the sun was west of south, Martin concluded.

Since Martin had been strafing north he ran hard for about twenty-five minutes south until he came to a field that had a herd of cows. The presence of the cows indicated he was not in German territory because soldiers would have eaten them up. He laid down on the ground near a fence trying to get his breath and looking around to see if anybody was watching him. After regaining his composure, he walked across the field to a small farmhouse. He found a middle-aged woman and a boy about 12 years old. The lady spoke enough English to ask him if he was hungry. He nodded his head and she cooked him two eggs and gave him some grappa (wine). It was Martin's good fortune that these people were part of a partisan group fighting on the side of the Allies.

Martin spent the next month eating and sleeping in a secret Yugoslavian camp high in the mountains with the partisan soldiers. When the DC-3 Transport finally came they arranged to fly him back to Italy where he joined his squadron and was then sent back to the United States.

Martin, who is now 80 years old, lives in Chicago following his retirement as an engineer for both the Park District and the City of Chicago.

"As a fighter pilot, you fight a war on your own." Martin said. "The only way you survive is by telling yourself every day: `I am the very best there is'."

The Honorable Charles E. Freeman, Justice of the Appellate Court of Illinois, administers the oath of office to the Honorable Harold Washington the forty-second Mayor of Chicago on April 29, 1983, as Cardinal Joseph Bernadin and former Mayor Jane Byrne look on.

CHAPTER IX

The Army Buck Private Who Became Mayor Of Chicago

Harold Washington was born in Chicago, Illinois at the Cook County Hospital at 11:11 p.m. on April 15, 1922. His father, Roy, was a lawyer and minister, and his mother, Bertha, was an intelligent, beautiful robust woman with a leaning toward pursuing a career in the theater.

In 1937, at DuSable High School, Harold opted to join the Reserve Officers Training Corps (ROTC) in place of taking gym because he felt that he got enough exercise practicing for track meets three to five hours daily. Although Harold didn't have any thought of ever going to war, he realized the ROTC training gave him a leg up on soldiering, in that he learned close-order drill and how to use many kinds of weapons ranging from a M-1 rifle to the 105 mm howitzer.

Harold dropped out of DuSable High School at age 17 in June of 1939 to join the Civilian Conservation Corps (CCC). Legislation establishing the CCC was pushed through Congress in 35 days after President Franklin D. Roosevelt was inaugurated on March 4, 1933. Unlike most of the young men Harold had to get his father's permission to join the Corps because he was underage. He also was from a middle class home, whereas the majority of the boys who signed up to work for a dollar a day plus three hots and a flop were from dirt poor families. Twenty-five of the thirty dollars earned monthly by the young men were allotments to help their depression-stricken families.

The Colored CCC boys served in segregated companies the same as their fathers had in World War I. Over 200,000 Negroes enrolled in the program between 1933 and 1942. They were all issued two dress uniforms, two work uniforms and two pairs of thick-soled tan Army shoes, plus a raincoat and a heavy weight Army brown winter coat. The Army Engineers constructed the camps which normally consisted of four barracks. Each barrack would accommodate 40 to 50 men. In addition there was a mess hall, a day room and officers' quarters. The Army ran the camps and the U.S. Forest Service supervised the boys' daily chores which were mostly manual. The tools used to accomplish their task were shovels, sledgehammers, double-edged axes and crosscut saws.

The CCC camps were run very much like the Army, minus close order drills and guns. The boys were awakened each morning by the sound of a bugler playing reveille. They lined up smartly at reveille for roll call in the morning and again for lowering the flag during retreat ceremony at sunset. The men made the chow line on time or missed the meal. G.I. Discipline governed the camps. Every camp had a sports program which included boxing, basketball, and baseball. Red Schoendienst, an infielder with the St. Louis Cardinal baseball team, who later became a Hall of Famer, served in the CCC in Illinois. A six month hitch in the Civilian Conservation Corps was about as much as Harold could digest.

Although the Germans had invaded Poland in September 1939 while Harold was still serving in the Civilian Conservation Corps, he did not envision that that action would possibly lead to him being called to arms to defend a "democracy" that was as foreign to him as "Alice in Wonderland."

Harold had not been out of the CCC camp a year before President Roosevelt signed into law the Selective Service Act, the first peace-time military draft in U.S. History. Within ten months following the attack on Pearl Harbor on December 7, 1941, the Army accelerated its call for Colored soldiers when the United States joined its Western allies in the invasion of North Africa. Harold was sworn into the Army in November 1942, and shipped out of Chicago from the Illinois Central Station at 12th and Michigan Avenue to Fort Custer, Michigan, near the city of Battle Creek, where he was processed through the all Colored 1609 Service Center.

Following the short stay at Fort Custer, Michigan, Pvt. Washington, his high school friend Theodore Davis and approximately 230 other Negro recruits were shipped by train in Jim Crow cars to Tonopah, Nevada for basic training. After a couple of days at Camp

Tonopah, an Army Air Force base, it became obvious to Washington and the other young soldiers that they had been shipped to the wrong camp because Tonopah had no infantry basic training facilities. The young recruits simply marked time in place for several months.

There was a soldier at Camp Tonopah with the surname of Shields who was a former Davis Cup tennis player. He asked Harold to help him recruit a boxing team to participate in the regional Golden Gloves finals, which were to be held in Reno, Nevada, about 100 miles from Camp Tonopah. Harold recruited a team of boxers in the upper six weights. Theodore 'Red' Davis, a former co-captain of the DuSable High School football team, was their heavyweight. Harold was the light heavyweight. Another guy whose name Harold could not recall was the middleweight. They trained hurriedly for about three weeks. The training was tough because the camp was approximately 6,000 feet above sea level, and none of the fellows were accustomed to exercising in that thin air.

Dawn finally broke after what seemed like an extremely long night of anticipation to Harold and his boxing team members. That was the day they were to make the trip to Reno, the gambling capital of America. They were told that they would be staying at the hotel. They didn't stay in a hotel room, but in a converted pantry or storage room where seven cots had been set up. Hotel food supplies had been stacked into a corner of the same room. The Colored soldiers had been moved around to the rear side of the hotel so fast they didn't know what was going on. For Harold and his boxing teammates this was a very humiliating experience. During the five days that they were there, they occasionally sneaked out the front door, which was the "FOR WHITES ONLY" entrance. What kind of way was that to treat American soldiers in uniform who were prepared to bleed to the very end for their country? Harold asked himself.

One day Red said, "Let's get out of this windowless pantry and go to Harrah's Gambling Casino." Harold wasn't much of a gambler. He played a little poker, but he wasn't going to play that kind of stuff out there. Anyway, they went to Harrah's and Red gambled a little bit. As Harold recalls, a fellow walked up to them as they were standing there watching a roulette wheel. He said, "No Colored allowed."

Harold said, "What?" He really didn't understand him at first. The floor man repeated, "No Colored allowed." Then Red said, "What did you say?"

So Harold and Red made a game out of it. And the floor man finally, in disgust, walked away. After that encounter, to make a long story short, they walked around in the casino with a sort of braggadocio strut for about 10 minutes and then split. It wasn't Harold's first encounter with prejudice; however, the racial wound was deeper because it was his first encounter with blatant racism as a soldier. Harold remembers after he got back to the pantry in the hotel, he was pretty upset about it. He wanted to get the hell out of town. But Shields calmed them down. They went on and fought in the tournaments. Red got beat pretty bad in his bouts. Harold lost one of his three bouts. Max Baer, the former heavyweight champion of the world, was the referee. Harold believed he would have had a better chance if Baer had not been the referee. Red obviously had gone along for the ride because he wasn't really a boxer.

On May 13, 1944 the battalion received orders to go to a deportation center near Seattle, Washington. Amid the blare of the military band, and the friendly Red Cross workers passing out hot coffee and donuts, a lot of tearful soldiers boarded the U.S.S. Grant for destination unknown.

The worst conditions that one could imagine about the troop ship U.S.S. Grant would, if voiced, be an understatement. The quarters were closet-like, dirty and depressing. The food was ill-prepared, unappetizing in appearance and the taste was no better. If it was the intent of the cook to make the men sick, he succeeded. The rocking motion of the ship caused many of the soldiers to suffer miserable bouts of seasickness.

Rumors of land being sighted on the seventh day at sea were thick as flies over an open garbage can. Then, on the morning of May 22, Diamond Head, the famous cliff-like structure at the entrance of Honolulu Harbor, loomed ahead. The land-starved soldiers hung over the rails of the ship like hungry dogs, eagerly anticipating their first look at a topless Hawaiian female wearing a skimpy grass skirt like those worn by Dorothy Lamour in her many South Sea Islands movies with Bing Crosby and Bob Hope. The men were really disappointed when they did not see a single girl when they debarked.

After six weeks in Hawaii they boarded a ship that was rumored to be going to Singapore. There were about 50 ships in the convoy, consisting mainly of LSTs, with mine sweepers and destroyer escorts playing a protective role. Secrecy necessitated a zigzag route, but the general direction was south by west toward the Solomon Islands.

On September 12, the men were assembled on the deck of the ship and given debarking orders. The task force was to bombard and invade the islands of Pelelieu and Angaur, in the Palau Group, which were situated at the Western extremity of the Caroline Islands.

The battalion continued its work until the middle of February 1945, when it was ordered to prepare to move to Guam, in the Marina Islands. After surmounting the inevitable transport impediments, the troops boarded the U.S.S. Johnson on February 27. The 1887th Engineer Aviation Battalion left behind it an impressive record embracing the completion of one runway, two taxiways and 93 hard stands; erection of two tank forms; and one transit hotel ready for use. When the U.S.S. Johnson plowed away from the shores of Angaur on the morning of February 28, the men on board realized that they were leaving the scene of a successful mission. Staff Sergeant Harold Washington made the following statement:

> Shortly after we reached Guam, I was made acting First Sergeant. It was one of those things. Talent was skimpy. I was the only Soil Technician in the entire area. They shuttled me from island to island periodically to test the soil. There had been a high mortality rate among Soil Technicians. I must have thought I was Emperor Jones and could only be wiped out with a silver bullet. (Washington roared with laughter after making that statement.) I did a great deal of structured. reading while I was overseas. I must have taken at least 30 correspondence courses. Every 90 days I would report to the company warrant officer, who was our resident

Mayor Harold Washington leads the St.Patrick's Day Parade.

The Mayor at his desk on the fifth floor of City Hall in Chicago.

teacher for correspondence courses, to take a test in his presence on the material I had completed. I took almost every course listed in the catalogues: history, literature, chemistry, and a great number of English courses. I didn't take any physics courses because the Soil Technician School had been an accelerated truncated course in physics. I devoured all that material. Some people drink and chew gum; I read. All of my correspondence credits were mailed back to DuSable High School by the company warrant officer.

On January 20, 1946, First Sergeant Harold Washington was discharged from the U.S. Army. Although Harold Washington frequently stated that he never dreamed of being Mayor of the City of Chicago, he never said that he was lacking the talent to do the job. Harold was elected Mayor on April 13, 1983, thirty-eight years after the end of World War II.

Lieutenant Colonel Harold Thatcher

CHAPTER X

The Black American Healers At Fort Huachuca, Arizona

Lieutenant Colonel Harold Thatcher graduated from the University of Minnesota Medical School in December 1929. Although he was in the top 25% of his class, his opportunities for internship were limited to thirteen out of several thousand hospitals nationwide because he was Black. The primary institutions available to Negroes were Provident Hospital in Chicago, Illinois; Freedmen's Hospital in Washington, D.C.; Harlem Hospital, New York; Lincoln Hospital, New York; Mercy Hospital, Philadelphia; St. Philips Hospital, Richmond, Virginia; Municipal Hospital No. 2, Kansas City, Missouri; Homer G. Philips Hospital and St. Mary's Infirmary, St. Louis, Missouri; Meharry Medical College, and Georgia W. Hubbard Hospital, in Nashville, Tennessee; Prairie View State College Hospital, in Prairie View, Texas; and Dillard University, New Orleans, Louisiana. The aforementioned institutions did not accept new interns until July 1 of each year.

In January of 1930 the chairman of the Department of Pediatrics at the University of Minnesota accepted a lateral transfer to the University of Chicago Hospital, in Chicago, Illinois. When he returned to Minnesota to visit his old clinic in early February he discovered that Thatcher had not been offered an internship. He promised to get Thatcher an internship at the University of Chicago if he would accept it. Thatcher accepted the offer like a hungry dog accepts red meat. Two weeks later he received a formal offer inviting him to come to Chicago.

As a result of the close affiliation between the University of Chicago and Provident Hospital during that period, Thatcher's first assignment was with Dr. Theodore K. Lawless, an internationally distinguished Black dermatologist who was the Senior Attending Physician at Provident Hospital. Lawless also taught three mornings a week at the Northwestern University School of Medicine in Chicago, Illinois.

Dr. Harold Thatcher and Dr. T.K. Lawless met for the first time on Monday morning, February 24, 1930. Dr. Thatcher describes the event: *I had never heard of Dr. Lawless; I did not know anything about him. I got up that Monday morning feeling as fresh as a bright yellow daisy, put on my white uniform, and paraded one block west, down the street to Provident Hospital, which fronted on East 51st Street across from*

Dr. Theodore K. Lawless
Dec. 6, 1892 - May 1, 1974

Washington Park between Forrestville and South Parkway. I found Dr. Lawless in a large out-patient room with two examining tables and four nurses. I said good morning, the nurses did not respond, and Dr. Lawless did not acknowledge my presence even with a nod of his head. I stood in the middle of the room and watched him examine several patients who appeared to be suffering from syphilis. After about an hour I began to feel that I was in the wrong room and in everybody's way. When I made a move to walk toward the door, Dr. Lawless broke the chilled silence of the room and said: 'Young man do you think you have seen enough of this sort of stuff?' I said: 'No, Sir!' Dr. Lawless snapped: 'You learn by looking you know.' I replied: 'Yes Sir!' The little man with the cold hazel eyes then gave me some smart talk and asked me if I knew how to give shots. I said: 'Yes Sir'. He then direct-ed that I set up a booth and table and give between 30 and 40 outpa-tient shots.

After I finished a one year internship under Dr. Lawless he arranged for me to go back to the University of Chicago for two more years. I could not legally practice medicine, but at night I would go *down to Dr. Lawless' private office at 43rd and South Parkway (Dr. Martin Luther King Drive) and help him. The first year he gave me $500.00. The next year he gave me a little bit more. He frequently reminded me that his office was the place where you learn things. He was both right and also very difficult to work with. He gave me hell all the time. It got so bad I called my father in Minneapolis and told him about the conditions under which I was working. My dad asked me why didn't I leave. I told him that Dr. Lawless was a very good doctor and possibly the best in his field. My dad's response was curt, he said: 'If the devil had something that I wanted, I would stick with him until I got it.'*

Dr. T. K. Lawless sent me to New York City for one year to study with some of his colleagues at the Harlem and Lincoln Hospitals. When I returned to Chicago he said he wanted me to come into practice with him. After negotiating a salary agreement I decided to stay with him and he promised to send me to Paris, France to study for another year. However, by September 1939 the German war machine had invaded Poland and started to move across Europe, that automatically vetoed any chance I had to study in Paris.

In October 1940 Henry L. Stimson, Secretary of War directed that Colored Medical Department officers be utilized only in units officered by Blacks, and that medical units with all whites remain lily-white in keeping with the World War I Jim Crow policy. Hospitals that served only Colored should be staffed exclusively by Colored personnel, including nurses. Colored and white medical officers could, if absolutely necessary, be used in the same hospital—provided that all supervising officers were white. There were Colored hospital wards at both Fort Bragg, North Carolina and Camp Livingstone, Louisiana. Both of them were staffed by Colored medical officers and nurses. The overall scheme of the Surgeon General's plan was to minimize physical contact between Colored and white officers in such areas as entertainment, eating and housing. Although Colored officers may have had top university credentials and proven leadership abilities, these were qualities that were never given any weight in the Jim Crow equation.

Initially, Colored nurses were sent to England to care for

Some of the nurses at Fort Huachuca, Arizona. Left to right: Bernice Batchelor, Los Angele
CA; Margaret A. Key, Philadelphia, PA; Bessie O. Hart, Steelton, PA; Ellen L. Robinson
Hackensack, NJ; Joan Hamilton, St.Louis, MO; Dorothy Branker, Bronx, NY; Lillian Mille
Richmond Heights, MO; Elena Townsend, Glen Cove, NY; Olive Lucas, Meadville, PA
Chrystallee Maxwell, Los Angeles, CA; Mary G. Tyler, St.Louis, MO.

Colored soldiers exclusively. However, when the Germans started
dropping bombs the Colored nurses were ordered to care for all soldiers regardless of race.

The 1940 Selective Service and Training Act found the Army
playing catch up on its need to draft an increasing number of Colored
doctors and dentists in order to meet its new 10% racial quota under
the Act. Dr. Thatcher was approached in the late winter of 1942 by
Truman K. Gibson Jr., Civilian Aide to The Secretary of War, to join
the Army and become part of a 1500 bed facility that was being built
at Fort Huachuca, Arizona. Thatcher initially was offered a commission as a First Lieutenant. He wrote back and told Truman Gibson
that he was going into another section of the Army because of some
special work he was doing. The War Department wrote back and said
he could come into the service as a Captain. Before Thatcher had a
chance to respond he received another letter saying that he could join

Colonel Midian O. Bousfield, Commanding Officer, Station Hospital Number 1, Fort Huachuca, Arizona.

the Fort Huachuca Hospital staff as a Major. The doctor signed on after receiving a third promotion in a period of 19 days without donning a military uniform.

When Thatcher reached Huachuca in the early summer of 1942 they were still building the 1500 bed medical facility for Colored soldiers. Thatcher and the other knowledgeable medical personnel had to order all of the equipment, such as hospital beds and the necessary machinery needed to run the hospital. It was better than a month before they could get into operation. However facility number 2, which was a 90 bed hospital, was in place for whites. It was used by white officers and enlisted men, their families and white civilian post personnel. When the word got around that the Colored doctors were better prepared credentially and by skills than the white doctors, white patients began coming to Thatcher, who had become known as an eminent skin specialist. All of the Colored Doctors were certified specialists at Station Hospital No. 1.

Thatcher was not pleased in having to work at a hospital that had not been completed, in addition to being stationed in the middle of a desert surrounded by mountains and thirty-four miles from the nearest railroad station. Although his immediate boss was a hometown friend, Colonel Midian O. Bousfield, Medical Director of the Supreme Liberty Life Insurance Company of Chicago, Special Health Director of the Julius Rosenwald (one of the founders of Sears) Fund and a member of the Chicago School Board, the Post Commander at Fort Huachuca was an unreconstructed southerner from Eastern Tennessee.

To add insult to injury the Post Commander had electrical barbed wire fences installed around the dormitories of white women who lived on the post, while no such protection was provided for Colored women living in the Jim Crow section of the Army base.

The Negro dormitories for married couples were unpainted plywood shacks that rivaled the worst slum housing in any back of the tracks ghetto. The living space per couple was seven feet square, each furnished with two Army cots and G. I. bedding.

The eleven couples who occupied the shelter all used the same bath facilities: one shower, one toilet stool, two enameled iron sinks that served as face basins, and a laundry tub, that was also used as a bathtub. There were no facilities for cooking. The monthly rent was $12.00.

In comparison, white couples had spacious private rooms, adequate sanitary and laundry facilities, bathtubs and showers. There were kitchens where they could prepare their own meals or have them prepared. White Army wives had no complaints other than the isolation of the post.

Captain Grant Reynolds of New York City and the Colored

Chaplin at Fort Huachuca made the following observation:

Negro soldiers will never forget the famous Hookers Girls (so called because during the Civil War, the female prostitutes who followed General John Hooker's soldiers were given the name-Hooker.) who served thousands of decent young men. The War Department will never be forgiven for allowing this disease laden practice to exist. The whores practiced their trade just south of the main entrance to the fort. They were housed in ramshackle huts, tents, and vermin-infested structures. This disgraceful activity did a thriving, though deadly, business in prostitution which took place right under the eyes of the Post Commander. Electric lights, running water, or any other signs of sanitation were entirely unknown. Yet this pesthole of venereal disease was allowed to flourish at the very front door of the home of the Negro soldier.

Reynolds further stated that:

Due to his deplorable environmental conditions the Negro, more than any other segment of the American population, has suffered from the ravages of social diseases. The War Department has gone to great expense and considerable effort to protect its soldiers from this deadly killer. Fort Huachuca Colored soldiers apparently did not come under the umbrella of this program.

The GU Wards (where venereal cases were treated) were over-taxed because the post authorities allowed their sex dens to operate at the front door to the living room of churchgoing, god-fearing Colored men and women who were forced to live in a desert fortress cut off from civilization because they volunteered or were drafted to fight and win a war to make democracy a reality on two fronts, at home for themselves and abroad for our European Allies.

Dr. Thatcher indicated that to control the venereal disease that was imported from Mexico, it would be necessary to send a team of doctors down to the Mexican border on weekends and require physical inspection of every soldier reentering the United States.

The following case related by Dr. Stephen Stanford of Philadelphia, the venereal disease control officer at Fort Huachuca, to Enoch Waters, his childhood friend and War Correspondent for the Chicago Defender. Waters was also the author of a history of the

Negro Press entitled the "American Diary", an excellent work.

Dr. Stanford tells the story about a G.I. who was a "clap" victim of a young "Good Time" girl for whom he expressed undying love.

Why didn't you use a rubber? the physician asked.

Oh I couldn't do a thing like that, sir. She ain't no whore and I am in love with her.

Maybe so, but you see she's got gonorrhea. What's her name? Where does she live?

I won't tell you, sir. She's a nice girl from a nice family. It wouldn't be right.

But she needs medical treatment which we can see that she gets. If she isn't treated, it will get worse and you can't make love to her anymore.

I'll handle it myself.

Besides, the doctor added as a second thought, *she might infect someone else.*

The young GI was indignant. *She loves only me.*

She don't mess around like some of the other girls.

Well, just to play safe you ought to use a rubber from now on.

I could never do that with her. It would be an insult.

Maybe so, but it would also keep her from getting pregnant. Did you ever think of that?

It wouldn't matter. We're going to be married.

The medical officer shook his head in disgust. *I don't know what to do about you guys.*

Fort Huachuca had the only fully staffed Colored hospital in the Army. Every one of the doctors was board certified in his specialty. As of February 1, 1943, 131 Negro nurses had been enrolled in the Army. Sixty-nine percent of them were stationed at Fort Huachuca. The 131 nurses were distributed as follows: Fort Huachuca 90, Camp Bragg 13, Camp Livingstone 15, Tuskegee 13.

Second Lieutenant Nora Green, a nurse at the station hospital of the Tuskegee Flying School, was brutally beaten by several white Montgomery police officers on September 12, 1942 because she boarded a bus that was otherwise occupied by whites. Both of her eyes were blackened and her nose was broken. She was thrown into a jail cell and charged with being intoxicated when it was known by her associates that she never drank anything stronger than a Coke.

Only 500 Colored nurses out of 50,000 served during World War II. The Navy had only four Colored nurses out of 11,000 during the same period. The Marines had none.

After Dr. Harold Thatcher was discharged from the Army in 1946, he renewed his practice of medicine with Dr. T. K. Lawless until Lawless died on May 1, 1974. Dr. Lawless respected and trusted Dr. Thatcher's judgement in that he made him co-executor of his estate with the former Continental Bank of Chicago.

Dr. Thatcher practiced medicine in the noble tradition of Dr. T. K. Lawless in that all patients, rich and poor, were treated alike on a first-come, first-served basis. Dr. Thatcher died in 1997.

Right: 1st Lieutenant Vernon Baker, the only Black living survivor of the seven Black World War II Medal of Honor recipients, and Jesse Brown, the Secretary of Veterans Affairs.

CHAPTER XI

Black Soldiers Died "Jim Crow" With Their Boots On

It is this author's opinion that African-Americans would have to be blindfolded and definitely on the wrong page in the world's history book not to be cognizant of the reality that they have been stigmatized from the womb to the tomb.

Fairness for Blacks is not a component in the American equation. My observation is a truism that applies to every level of opportunity where Black folk are involved from the streets to the executive suites. A classic example of being left out of the equation was exemplified in bold relief in the American Military during World War II where fairness managed to escape Blacks even after death.

One million two hundred thousand Blacks served in the Armed Forces during the World War II years between 1941 to 1945 and only seven were awarded the prestigious Medal of Honor for valor fifty-three years after the event. 1st Lt. Vernon J. Baker, 76 of St. Maries, Idaho, was the only one of seven men who was still around to smell the sweet scent of the roses at the White House ceremony when President William Jefferson Clinton made giant steps toward correcting an overdue wrong on January 13, 1997. The other six Medals of Honor were awarded posthumously. Not a single Tuskegee Airman, or Marine was recommended for the Medal of Honor for their heroic service in the European or Pacific theater during World War II.

The other six Black soldiers who were recognized posthumously as distinguishing themselves on the battlefield during the Big War were Staff Sgt. Edward A. Carter Jr., of Los Angeles, California, 1st Lt. John R. Fox of Cincinnati, Ohio, Pfc. Willy F. James Jr., of Kansas City, Missouri, 1st Lt. Charles L. Thomas of Detroit, Michigan, Pvt. George Watson of Birmingham, Alabama, and Staff Sgt. Ruben Rivers of Hotulka, Oklahoma.

The recognition for the seven came after a long running political tug of war with the military brass at the Pentagon. The battle for recognition was spearheaded by fellow World War II Veterans and their families who saw their denial of being honored as racist and unfair. There had been 433 white WWII recipients of the Medal of Honor but not a single Black.

Among those vigorously supporting the contention for a Black receiving the Medal of Honor was former Captain David Williams, the white commander of Company A of the All-Black 761St Tank Battalion. The Captain witnessed Staff Sgt. Ruben Rivers lead a tank attack on German positions near Bourgaltroff, France in November, 1944, despite his having been afflicted with severe leg wounds. Rivers died in that attack on that cold November morning. Captain Williams was convinced that if Rivers had been white, he would have been honored promptly instead of 53 years after he was killed. Captain Williams had nominated Rivers for the Medal of Honor the day after the young soldier died at age 25 several days before the Thanksgiving holiday in 1944. In reality there are no holidays in hell.

Vernon Baker the only surviving World War II Medal of Honor recipient shared the following remarks about his battle-front experience, in 1945 on the 5th and 6th of April near Viareggio, Italy:

When my company was stopped by the concentrated fire from several machine-gun emplacements, I crawled to one position and destroyed it, killing three Germans. Continuing forward, I attacked an enemy observation post and killed its two occupants. With the aid of one of my men, I attacked two more machine-gun nests, killing or wounding the four enemy soldiers occupying those positions. I then covered the evacuation of the wounded personnel of my company by occupying an exposed position and drawing the enemy's fire.

On the following night, I voluntarily led a battalion advance through enemy minefields and heavy fire towards the division objective. My fighting spirit and daring leadership was an inspiration to my men and exemplified the highest traditions of the United States Armed Forces.

I was the only Black officer in the 92nd Infantry Division in the Mediterranean Theater of Operations to receive the Distinguished

Service Cross, which is the Army's second highest medal for bravery, I added it to my Bronze Star and Purple Heart. Eighteen of my 25 men died on that hill. They were good men. Like I have always said, they never knew how good they really were.

During battle I always kept in the forefront of my mind the lessons taught me in the Officer Candidate School. Remember the mission. Set the example. Keep going until you bleed.

I can look back now and say if it ever happens to anybody else, just hang in there by your toenails. I can look back at my life and say I hung in there.

They had a new set of white officers when the battle for the hills began. My company commander, a white captain, was with us at the start, but as the casualties mounted, he told me he was going back down the hill for reinforcements.

When he left I told him rather sarcastically 'OK Captain, I'll see you later.' I really didn't expect him to return, and he didn't.

The reinforcements never came. The Captain had deserted his Black Troops.

A photographer from the 92nd Division saw me as I came off the hill that second morning. He said he saw me sitting there vomiting my guts out. I said, 'Why didn't you take my picture?'

He said, 'I'm sorry I didn't.'

The captain survived without a scratch. He told Colonel Murphy that we had all been eliminated up there on the hill. When he left he didn't expect us to survive. I was told by a professor who was a military historian at Shaw University, in Raleigh, North Carolina that my company commander had recommended himself for the Medal of Honor way back in 1945. But he didn't get it.

Dempsey J. Travis, the author, states that he did not get a Purple Heart when he was shot 3 times in 1943 at Camp Shenango. *All I got was a red Good Conduct Medal. On the other hand following the War, I was subsequently told that I was not entitled to any kind of compensation for my imagined service connected injuries. I had been told all of my life that you can not beat Uncle Sam, therefore I dropped the matter after I filed for a disability claim shortly after being discharged from the Army on February 2, 1946.*

Sergeant Dempsey J. Travis

My disabilities were never discussed outside of the family until I accidently met a man who turned out to be Jesse Brown, the Secretary of Veterans Affairs who had tagged along with his sister, who is the wife of Chicago Police Superintendent Terry Hillard, to inspect a model home that I had built in one of my new developments.

Secretary Brown of Veterans Affairs had lost part of his arm in the Vietnam conflict. This gave cause for me to discuss my war injuries with Brown. The Secretary found my story a bit hard to fathom. Therefore, I asked the Secretary to read a chapter in "Views From The Back Of The Bus During WWII", a book in which I had documented my case. After reading the chapter in the book, the Secretary shook his head in disbelief. He then said, 'Do you mind if I look up your case when I go back to Washington?' I answered, 'No, I don't mind at all.' The Secretary then said, 'Give me your army serial number and I will have somebody examine your records.' I retorted, 'My serial number is 36393756.'

Several months passed before I received a letter from the Office of Veterans Affairs asking for additional information. Then there was another lapse of time before I received another request for information.

On May 28, 1997 I received a letter from the Department of Veterans Affairs. It read,

Dear Mr. Travis:

We made a decision on your compensation claim.

We have found that there was a clear and unmistakable error in the rating decision dated April 22, 1946. Based on the results of the Administrative review dated April 22, 1997, (which was 51 years later) we have found the following disabilities are service connected.. Attached herewith are the conditions and percentages of your disability.

We used a "combined rating table" to decide how disabled you are. The percentages in this table are set by regulation. Your overall or combined disability evaluation is 30%.

Sincerely yours,

Dean Kurtz
Service Center Manager

In addition to the final letter, the author Dempsey J. Travis received several brown government envelopes containing checks totaling $75,000 plus notice of a lifetime pension for both he and his wife.

How long is a Black man's life expectancy at age 77? Not Long! According to the latest 1999 statistics, World War II soldiers are dying at the rate of 1,000 a day, if a Black man dies at the age of 65, he died on time.

Acknowledgments

A good coach never changes the front line of a winning team. Therefore, with great pride, I salute the following players: My wife, Moselynne Travis, the motivator; Ruby Davis, senior researcher; Jewell E. Diemer; Ken Kitti, jacket and book designer; and Cheryl English.

Also, a special thanks to:

Archie Motley - Chicago Historical Society.

Frank C. Bacon, Jr. - Brigadier General, U.S.A. Retired.

Charles E. Fleming - Colonel, ARNG

Photo Credits

Lloyd E. Wheeler, III.

Mayor Harold Washington.

1st Lieutenant Robert Martin.

Captain David W. Pelkey.

Retired Lieutenant Colonel Earl E. Strayhorn.

Lieutenant Colonel Harold Thatcher.

Jesse Brown, Secretary of Veterans Affairs.

Alderman Louis B. Anderson, family.

The Sengstacke family.

Bibliography

Interviews:

Interviews by Dempsey J. Travis With Individuals Who
Had World War I Experience As Soldiers and Civilians

Alexander, Frank, age 80, August 12, 1972

Baker, Elmor, age 92, June 12, 1977

Browne, William Y. , admitted to being over age 74, July 26, 1977

Crawford, Joe, age 71, December 27, 1980

Dickerson, Earl B. , age 90, August 21, 1977 and various dates in 1978, 79, 80, and 81.

Duster, Alfreda M. Barnett, age 73, July 10, 1977

Evans, Lovelyn J. , age 82, August 4, 1977

Freeman, Oscar, age 80, June 15, 1977

Gibson, T. K. , age 87, September 10, 1969

Grinnell, Anna Mary, age 94, July 29, 1977 and August 21, 1977

Harris, George S. , age 79, September 17, 1977

Herrick, Mary, age 84, and various dates in 1979, 80 and 81

Hill, Richard, age 80, June 10, 1969

Lewis, Dr. Julian, age 85, July 19, 1981

Mead, Ripley B. , Sr. , age 79, June 10, 1969

Overton, Ida, age 80, May 16, 1981

Ragland, John, age 96, April 13, 1980

Robinson, Mae, age 71, June 12, 1977

Smith, Dr. Bishop, age 70, June 15, 1969

Smith, Dr. Reginald, age 86, June 15, 1969

Travis, Mittie, age 80, June 12, 1977

Wheeler, Lloyd III, age 72, August 14, 1977

Williams, Ira W. , age 92, August 10, 1977

Woodard, Oneida Daniels, about 80 years old, August 4, 1977

Interviews by Dempsey J. Travis with Persons
Who Had World War II Experience As Soldiers

Black, Corporal Timuel D. , 8/30/94, 9/30/94

Brazier, Staff Sergeant Arthur, 11/15/94

Campbell, Staff Sergeant Wendell, 9/9/94

Coleman, Seaman 1st Class David C. , 8/9/94

Cousins, 1st Lieutenant William, 3/15/91

Deas, 1st Lieutenant Milton B. , 9/9/94, 1/2/95

Gardner, Sergeant Edward G. , 9/6/94

Gardner, Staff Sergeant Frank, 8/23/94

Gibson, Civilian Aide Truman K. Jr. , 7/6/94, 12/4/94

Hervey, 1st Lieutenant Henry P. , 8/26/94

Johnson, Judge E. C. 8/29/94

Jones, Third Class Petty Officer Mark, 9/30/94

Kirkpatrick, Captain Felix, 8/29/94, 9/2/94, 9/29/94

Leighton, Captain George N. , 9/22/94, 1/23/95

Long, Staff Sergeant Alvin C. , 9/12/94

Martin, Captain Robert, 9/8/94

Myles, Corporal Eddie, 8/20/94, 10/10/94

Pelkey, Captain David, 1/9/95, 1/12/95

Rogers, Captain John W. , 9/1/94, 11/27/94

Russell, Ensign Harvey, 9/25/94

Skinner, Corporal Clementine, 9/29/94

Stewart, Private Wilborn, 8/25/94

Strayhorn, Lieutenant Earl, 8/22/94, 1/9/95

Taylor, 1st Lieutenant George, 9/1/94

Taylor, Corporal Raymond, 5/30/94, 9/30/94, 8/30/95

Taylor, 1st Lieutenant Welton, 2/20/95, 2/22/95, 9/27/94, 10/4/94

Thatcher, Lieutenant Colonel Harold W. , 9/29/94, 10/13/94

Thomas, 1st Sergeant Joseph, 8/19/94

Thompson, 1st Lieutenant Bill, 9/1/94

Washington, 1st Sergeant Harold, 4/23/83, 4/31/83, 5/31/83, 1/2/84, 5/12/84,
5/19/84, 7/14/84, 8/16/84, 4/18/85, 8/12/85, 9/22/86, 10/15/86, 10/18/86

Westbrook, 1st Lieutenant Shelby, 9/14/94

Wheeler, Sergeant Lloyd, 9/6/94, 12/19/94, 12/21/94

Williams, 1st Lieutenant James B. , 4/28/90, 12/7/94, 12/19/94

Books

Aptheker, Herbert, The Negro People in the United States 1933-1945, Citadel Press, Secaucus, New Jersey, 1974.

A Historical and Pictorial View of the National Guard and Naval Militia of the State of Illinois, Army and Navy Publishing Company Inc. , Baton Rouge, Louisiana, 1940.

The Negro In Chicago: A Study of Race Relations and A Race Riot in 1919, Arno Press and New

York Times, New York, NY 1968.

John P. Davis, Editor, The American Negro, Negro Reference Book, Prentice Hall , Inc. , Englewood Cliffs, NJ 1969.

Black Americans In Defense of Our Nation, Department of Defense, Washington, D. C. 1982.

Franklin, John Hope, From Slavery To Freedom, Alfred A. Knopf, New York, NY 1947.

Greene, Robert Ewell, Black Defenders of America, 1775- 1973, Johnson Publishing Company, Inc. , Chicago, IL 1974.

Herrick, Mary J. , The Chicago Schools, Sage Publication, Beverly Hills, CA. , 1971.

Lee, Ulysses, The United States Army in World War II Special Studies: The Employment of Negro Troops Washington, D. C. Office of the Chief of Military History the United States Army, 1966.

Majors, Gerri With Doris E. Saunders, Black Society, Johnson Publishing Company Inc. , Chicago, IL 1976.

Scott, Emmett J. , Official History of The American Negro in the World War, Arno Press and The New York Times, New York, NY 1969.

The Chicago Commission on Race Relations, The Negro In Chicago, The University of Chicago Press, Chicago, IL 1922.

Travis, Dempsey J. , Views From The Back Of The Bus During WWII and Beyond, Urban Research Press Inc. , Chicago, IL 1975.

Travis, Dempsey J. , The Autobiography of Black Chicago, Urban Research Press Inc. , Chicago, IL 1981.

Travis, Dempsey J. , The Autobiography of Black Politics, Urban Research Press Inc. , Chicago, IL 1987.

Travis, Dempsey J. , Harold The People's Mayor, Urban Research Press Inc. , Chicago, IL 1989.

Tuttle, William A. Jr. , et al, A People and A Nation: A History of the United States, University of Kansas et al, Houghman, Lipman Company, Boston, MA 1982.

Tuttle, William M. Jr. , Race Riot Atheneum, New York, NY 1977.

Waters, Enoch, P. , American Diary, Path Press Inc. , Chicago, IL 1987.

NEWSPAPER ARTICLES

Greatest Military Entertainment and Ball, The Chicago Defender, January 29, 1910

The 8th Regiment Ball Most Brilliant in Years, The Chicago Defender, February 19, 1910.

Eighth Infantry Illinois National Guard, The Chicago Defender, April 30, 1910.

Doctor Wesley, The Chicago Defender, May 28, 1910.

Great 15th Anniversary Celebration, The Chicago Defender, September 24, 1910.

Capt. Louis B. Anderson, The Chicago Defender, May 11, 1912.

Grand Military Reception and Ball, The Chicago Defender, June 1, 1912.

The "Eighth's" Field Day Exercises, The Chicago Defender, July 27, 1912.

Eighth Regiment Ball, The Chicago Defender, December 27, 1913.

The 8th Illinois National Guard's New Home, The Chicago Defender, May 9, 1914.
Eighth Regiment Off Tonight For Camp Lincoln, The Chicago Defender, July 25, 1914.
"Down State"; Boys of 8th Regiment Are Good Soldiers, The Chicago Defender, August 8, 1914.
Cornerstone Laying of 8th Regiment Armory Event in Race History, The Chicago Defender, October 17, 1914.
New Armory, 8th Regiment I. N. G., The Chicago Defender, February 6, 1915.
Eighth Regiment Now Quartered at Camp Lincoln, The Chicago Defender, August 7, 1915.
Eighth Regiment Hard At Work At Camp Lincoln, The Chicago Defender, August 14, 1915.
The Brink of War U. S. Draws Color Line, The Chicago Defender, August 28, 1915.
"Army Rushes Plans For All-Negro Division; Issues Call For Volunteers":, Chicago Defender, December 20, 1941.
"Jim Crow Draft Call" Afro-American, December 5, 1942.
"Sgt. Deas Promoted to Lieutenant", Chicago Defender, February 6, 1943.
"General Stockton Reminds Soldiers They Were Slaves", Afro-American, August 14, 1943.
"Chicago Men In Armed Service", Chicago Defender, October 9, 1943.
"73 GIs Convicted For Hawaii Mutiny", Chicago Defender, February 3, 1945.
"General Bradley Okays Jim Crow Rule In Dixie", Chicago Defender, January 12, 1946.
Welcome to the 30s, Chicago Daily News, March 8-9, 1975.
Welcome to the 30s, Chicago Daily News, March 10, 1975.
The History of the 184th Field Artillery, Chicago Defender, July 8, 1995.
Chicago Renaissance Revisited, Chicago Defender, September 12, 1998.
Provident Hospital Revives Rich History, Chicago Sun-Times, November 2, 1998.
Herbert Young, Obituaries, New York Times, April 28, 1999.

MAGAZINES

The Eighth Illinois Infantry Returns, Half-Century Magazine, November, 1916.
America Enters World War I, Half-Century Magazine, April, 1917.
East St. Louis Riot, Half-Century Magazine, October, 1917.
Selling Out The Race, Half-Century Magazine, February, 1919.
The Return of the "Black Devils", Half-Century Magazine, March, 1919.
Big Hearted Chicago, Half-Century Magazine, April, 1919.
Negro Life In Chicago, Half-Century Magazine, May, 1919.
The Race Riots and the Press, Half-Century Magazine, May, 1919.
The Race Riot In Chicago, Half-Century Magazine, September, 1919.
Africa Unbenefited By The World War, Half-Century Magazine, September, 1919.
French Condemn Americans Treatment of Colored Soldiers, Half-Century Magazine, October, 1919.
By What Name Shall The Race Be Known, Half-Century Magazine, November, 1919.

"Winfred Lynn Case Again: Segregation in the Armed Forces", The Social Service Review Magazine, December 1944.

World War II Ends, Half-Century Magazine, August, 1945.

Negro Heroes of the Civil War, Negro Digest, February 1966.

The Buffalo Soldiers, Negro Digest, July, 1967.

"The Brownsville Incident" Ebony Magazine, March 1973.

"The Good War", Chicago Tribune Magazine, December 1, 1991.

JOURNALS & PAMPHLETS

"The Negro and World War II", Negro Handbook, 1944.

"The Eighth Illinois" Negro History Bulletin, Vol. 7, April, 1944.

Blacks in Blue - Chicago History The Chicago Historical Society, Vol-III Number 12, 1954.

Blacks and U. S. Wars, National Urban League, Inc. 1976.

"Conspiracy to Discredit the Black Buffaloes: The 92nd Infantry in World War II", Journal of Negro History, Winter/Spring 1987.

Chicago Tribune - Markers of Distinction City of Chicago - Chicago Department of Cultural Affairs, 1998.

The Chicago Military Academy Bronzeville, City of Chicago, Chicago Public Schools, 1998.

MEMOIRS

Memoirs, From the Scrapbook of Alderman Louis B. Anderson

ARTICLES

March on the Conventions Movement For Freedom Now, Chicago Chapter-NAACP, July 1, 1960

Roster - Officers of 370th Infantry Regiment, by Anthony L. Powell.

INDEX

Ku Klux Klan - 15, 16, 38

Kurtz, Dean - 114

Lake Michigan - 20

Lamont, Daniel - 3

Langford, Lawrence - 81

Laughton, Charles - 79

Lawless, Theodore K. - 101, 102, 108

Lincoln, Abraham - 2, 16

Lincoln Hospital, New York, N. Y. - 100

Lockbourne Army Air Force Base, Ohio - 82

Lorraine Offensive - 10

Los Angeles, CA - 103, 110

Lowden, Frank O. - 16

Lucas, Olive - 103

Lunceford, Jimmie - I

Madden, Martin B. - 2, 3, 6

Marina Island - 96

Marshall, George C. - 66

Marshall, Thurgood - 41

Martin, Henry - 83 - 90

Martin, Robert - 83 - 90, 115

Masonic Lodge, Chicago, IL - 27

Masons, The - 7

Massachusetts Institute of Technology - 59

Maxwell, Chrystalee M. - 103

Mc Nair, Lesley J. - 81

McArthur, Douglas - 56

McCormick, Medill - 39

Meadville, PA - 103

Medal of Honor - 110-112

Mediterranean Theater of Operation - 111, 112

Mercy Hospital, Philadelphia, PA. - 100

Mexican Border - 16

Mexican Claims Commission - 39

Military Police (MP's) - 80

Military High School Academy, Chicago, IL - II

Miller, Lucille B. - 103

Minor, Byron - 81

Montgomery, Alabama - 85

"Mood Indigo" (Song) - 60

"Moonglow" (Song) - 60

Moore, Henrietta - 42

Moore, Loring B. - 40

Motley, Archie - 115

Municipal Hospital, Kansas City MO., - 100

Naples, Italy - 82

National Association for the Advancement of Colored People (NAACP) - 56

National Industrial Recovery Act (NIRA) - 61

National Recovery Act (NRA) - 58

Negro Press - 107

Nevada, Reno - 94

New Deal - 60

"No Colored Allowed" - 94, 95

North Africa Campaign - 81

Northwestern University School of Medicine, Evanston, IL - 42, 101

"Now's the Time to Fall in Love" (Song) - 52

Oakland Square Theater, Chicago, IL - 39

Oakwood Cemetery, Chicago, IL - 74

Office of Veterans Affairs - 109, 113, 114

Officer Candidate School - 67, 112

Oise - Aisne Offensive - 10

"On the Sunny Side of the Street" (Song) - 60

Overton, Anthony, Chicago, IL - I

Paris, France - 16

Patton, George S. - 56

Pearl Harbor - 62, 66, 77, 93

Pelelieu Islands - 96

Pelkey, David W. - 65-74, 81, 115

Pentagon, Washington, D. C. - 111

Pershing, John J. - 13, 30

Petersburg, VA. - 42

Pickens, William (Dean) - 43 - 47

Pitts, Anderson F. - 67, 68, 77, 78

Pittsburgh Courier Newspaper - 14

Playboy Magazine - 53

Post Exchange (PX) - 73

Prairie View State College, Houston, TX. - 100

Provident Hospital, Chicago, IL 100, 101

Public Works Program (PWA) - 61

Pullman Porters - 58, 59

Purple Heart - 112

Pythians, The - 7

Racism - 13

Rand, Sally - 55

Randolph, A. Philip - 41

Randolph, John - 27

Rantoul, IL - 76

Ray, Marcus H. - 67, 69 - 71, 80, 81

Raymond Elementary School, Chicago, IL - 16, 17

Rector, John A. - 81

Redding, Otis - 69

Republican Party - 59

Reserve Officers Training Corps (ROTC) - 92

Reynolds, Grant - 105

Richmond Heights, MO. - 103

Rivers, Ruben - 110

Roanoke, VA - 27

Robeson, Paul - 41

Robinson, Ellen L. - 103

Roosevelt, Franklin D. - 57, 60, 62, 92, 93

Rose, Edna - 39

Rosenwald, Julius - 105

Samson, Charles L. - 26

Santiago, Cuba - 3, 4

Schoendienst, "Red" - 93

Sears Roebuck, Chicago, IL - 105

Seattle, Washington - 95

Second Ward/Chicago, IL - 7, 40, 42

Secretary of Veterans Affairs - 113

Selective Service Act of 1940 - 103

Sengstacke Family - 115

Shaw University, Raleigh N. C. - 112

Small, Len - 39

Solomon Islands - 96

"Sophisticated Lady" (Song) - 60

South Sea Islands - 95

Southern Democrats - 59

Spanish American War - 3

St. Gobain Forest - 10

St. Louis Cardinal Baseball Team - 93